MY
BROWN
BABY

MY BROWN BABY

On the Joys and Challenges of Raising African American Children

Denene Millner

A Denene Millner Book

BOLDEN

AN Agate IMPRINT

CHICAGO

Printed in the United States

My Brown Baby
ISBN 13: 978-1-57284-212-0
ISBN 10: 1-57284-212-1
ebook ISBN 13: 978-1-57284-793-4
ebook ISBN 10: 1-57284-793-X

First printing: March 2017

10 9 8 7 6 5 4 3 2 1   17 18 19 20

Bolden Books is an imprint of Agate Publishing. Agate books are available
in bulk at discount prices.

agatepublishing.com

For my Girlpies, Mari and Lila, who taught my heart to sing . . .

Mama exhorted her children at every opportunity to
"jump at de sun." We might not land on the sun,
but at least we would get off the ground.
—ZORA NEALE HURSTON

As their mother, your job is to keep the kids from killing
their fool selves.
—BETTYE MILLNER

CONTENTS

RAISING THEM UP:
The Nuts and Bolts of Parenting Black Children

BEYOND THE LIGHTS:
Loosening Pop Culture's Hold on Black Children

HAIR STORIES:
The Joys, Pains, and Politics of Black Children's Kinky Curls

THE SOULS OF BLACK FOLK:
Parenting Beyond Stereotypes

THEY'LL WEAR THE ARMOR:
Black Children and Racism

THE MARTYRS:
On Black Children, Race, and Lives That Mattered

MY BROWN BABY MATTERS:
The Politics of Raising Black Children

MOTHER LOVE

INTRODUCTION

I STARTED *MyBrownBaby* on a whim in September 2008, back when the Barack Obama vs. John McCain presidential election was in full gear and the pregnancy of Sarah Palin's teen daughter, Bristol, was setting the news cycles on fire. My first post questioned how the pregnancy of li'l Miss Bristol would have been viewed if she were, oh, say, a black teenager—a conversation that was being had by black moms everywhere, but was virtually ignored in every news story/blog post/TV analysis from here to Wasilla.

It was an observation that combined the two things I love writing about most—black folk and parenting—and I thought it a fitting debut post for *MyBrownBaby*, a space I created for African American moms looking to lend their critical but all-too-often ignored voices to the national parenting debate.

MyBrownBaby is irreverent. Funny. Full of posts that make you think. Maybe even say, "Amen!" because it reminds you of what's going on behind your closed door, with your family. It's a place where African American parents and parents of black children and their opinions matter, and are heard, respected, and revered. For their poignancy and strength. For their intelligence and authenticity.

Because they deserve it.

Of course, *MyBrownBaby* does not come without its detractors; apparently, the word "brown" in my blog title makes some people—mainly white women—feel some kind of way about my posts, subject matter, and intent, and some are even bold enough to stomp onto the site questioning why, if "everyone wants to be celebrated and recognized as 'equal,'" I would "segregate" myself with a blog about skin color.

Let me be very clear: I've been a working journalist since my senior year in high school, and in my lengthy career, I've covered everything from murder and politics to entertainment and parenting and everything in between with great joy, care, and skill. Not every story of mine has been about black people. One of these days I'll give you the lowdown on the time I interviewed George Clooney in a swanky New York City hotel, or what it was like to hold a miniature tape recorder in former New York City mayor Rudolph Giuliani's face during a mayoral press conference.

But, I'm an African American mom with brown babies, and I take great pleasure in writing about the issues moms of color and mothers of children of color face as we raise our kids. And while I happily cosign the idea that at the base of it, we moms all want the same things for our children—for them to be happy, healthy, smart, kind, honest, trustworthy, successful human beings—we simply do not all parent the same, and there absolutely *are* issues that I deal with as an African American mom that white moms would never have to think about if they're not raising a brown child.

A "for instance": once I wrote about what it takes to groom and style a little black girl's hair (a post inspired, ironically, by a raging debate about whether Angelina Jolie does a good enough job combing her black daughter's hair). Wild guess, but I'm going to go on ahead and assume that styling coarse, curly hair is not something most white moms with white children think about, like, ever. But as the mother of two black girls, I have to think about it *every day*. Still, I can't look for information on this simple, everyday topic in most parenting books/magazines/websites/ blogs that proclaim to be for and about *all moms* to get the valuable info I need to avoid damaging my daughters' thick, curly manes.

Similarly, it's hard to find, in mainstream media, information on how to cope with the fear that comes with raising a super smart, super sweet, super handsome, super big, super black teenage son in a society full of folks who still judge black boys by the color of their skin, rather than the content of their character.

Or how to fight against the long-held notion in our community that breastfeeding babies is nasty—or worse, something that only white moms do.

Need I go on?

See, I write about African Americans not to point fingers at white moms, but to help black ones. Is this segregating myself? Nope. It's providing a service for us moms who *need* the information but can't find it or who just want someone to commiserate with them—help us sort through the beautiful struggle that comes with being black parents in America.

This is done with open arms, a lot of love, and the deep belief that though we may come from separate places and have different backgrounds, we are ALL moms who want the same things for our families, and especially for our children.

My Brown Baby: The Joys and Challenges of Raising African American Children is a collection of my favorite posts over the last eight years—pieces that speak to not only my journey as a mother, but the collective experiences of African American mothers, our joys, our fears, our sorrows, and our triumphs. Though some were written when my girls were just wee-bits, they are still heartfelt to me, and relevant to moms who are thinking about having children, who are new moms, or who are veterans in this motherhood journey. Choosing the best among eight years of text was no easy task: with nearly two thousand posts on my server, I was charged with pouring through each piece with the specific goal of figuring out which among them held the most heft and meaning across the span of motherhood, from pregnancy consideration and conception, to birth and early childhood, to the special role we take on as parents of teens and tweens. Each stage, after all, is an inevitable part of parenting, if we're lucky enough to make it through each round. Still, I wanted this book to be more than just the stages of parenting; I wanted it to be the very essence of *black* parenting. To that end, once I organized the posts by stages of parenting, I chopped and screwed them into topics unique and important to parents raising children of color, the most significant among them being racism and its effect on how others treat us, and how we protect ourselves and our babies from the problems that come with it; pop culture and its hold on how we see ourselves and interact within a society that sees "brown," "curvy," and "kinky-haired" as less than; the politics of nurturing, growing, and loving our children's natural hair; what it takes to face off against (and, in some cases, embrace) stereotypes saddled on black parents and our children; the politics of black parenting; and, on a more personal level, learning how to love, respect, and protect ourselves through it all. What emerges is a powerful essay collection—equal parts personal narrative, observation, and analysis—that speaks to the totality of what it's meant to be a modern, thoughtful, engaged black parent in America.

Read these essays with an open mind and you just might see perspectives on family, motherhood, love, and relationships that are fresh and different and interesting and familiar or eye opening.

Beautifully human.

BIRTHING WHILE BLACK

The Journey to Motherhood

CHAPTER 1

My Escort into Motherhood

I WAS A YOUNG REPORTER WHEN I MET HER— full of energy, I had a flat stomach, still 120 pounds soaking wet, still eating popcorn and rainbow sherbet for dinner. Despite having awesome health insurance, I'd gone years without seeing a doctor of any kind. When you're in your 20s, lying on a table with your legs up in the air while a total stranger peers at and feels all over your goodies is never at the top of your list of things to do.

But she insisted I come see her. A woman, she said, needs to keep track of her health—no matter how uncomfortable, no matter how busy, no matter how fearful, no matter what. And so I called her office and made an appointment and not even two weeks later, I was on Dr. Hilda Hutcherson's table, having my lady parts examined.

I'd submitted to nurse practitioners at local clinics when I was a college student; how else to get low-cost birth control without involving your parents? But Hilda was my first real gynecologist. Work brought her to me and me to her; as a young features writer for the *New York Daily News*, I was searching for a story to whip up for Mother's Day, and her book, *Having Your Baby: For the Special Needs of Black Mothers-To-Be, from Conception to Newborn Care*, just happened to be floating around the newsroom; it just made sense for me to write a piece about the joys and challenges of black mothers. Mind you, I didn't have any babies of my own—wasn't even thinking about being a mother anytime soon. But even then, back in 1997, a full two years before I would have a baby of my own, giving a voice to and telling the stories of African American mothers was important to me. Necessary. Witness what Hilda told me when, for a *Daily News* Mother's Day story I penned about her back in the mid-1990s, I asked her how she balanced a thriving Upper East Side practice, writing books, and a husband and four kids. Here's how she answered:

> It's a tradition of mothering that goes back hundreds of years," Hutcherson offers simply. "I think that black women have always been valiant for their ability to do multiple things at the same time. They mother their children and take care of other people's children, sometimes breast-feeding your baby and their babies, too . . . take care of the household, raise children, be a wife, work hard for little recognition and pay, and do it all well on limited means.
>
> I think that was very hard for my mother, her mother and other African American women but somehow they managed. I was always taught that I could, too.

Sure, some could argue that the civil rights movement and Martin Luther King, Jr. made it so that, today, there's really no difference between, say, an African American mother with a career and a white counterpart with all the same responsibilities. But that counterpart probably wouldn't have thought about it for longer than two minutes.

Most African American women will tell you there's an added struggle with being a black mother—an extra pile of junk in the trunk. There are the stereotypes (all black mothers are single and on welfare), the hardships (pay rates, though better today, are still among the lowest for black women) and the racism (people treat her differently or badly because she's black).

It is our story. Our truth. Hilda's too. Still, Hilda soldiered on, and managed well. Since then, she's become a leading authority on women and sexuality, having written three books geared toward helping us be smarter about and get more pleasure from sex; worked as a sexual health columnist at *Essence* and *Glamour* magazines and served as an expert on the *Today* show and in *O, The Oprah Magazine*; served as a clinical professor of obstetrics and gynecology and as the associate dean of the Office of Diversity and Multicultural Affairs at Columbia University's College of Physicians and Surgeons; and, through it all, ushered four babies through childhood.

While Hilda's fancy titles, Oprah connections, and sexual empowerment talks are impressive, none of them can compare to why I love her. It was she, after all, who, along with my husband, was present on one of the most important days of my life—she whose hands guided my first baby into the land of the living.

The crazy part is that she wasn't even supposed to be in my delivery room. Hilda was on vacation when her colleague, worried that my baby would be too big to push through my teeny birth canal, called me in to the hospital to be induced. Of course, it was a tad heartbreaking that Hilda wouldn't be in the delivery room with me, but I'd met all except one of the partners in her practice, and all of them were awesome so I wasn't too worried . . . until the one doctor who'd never met me showed up to my labor room to introduce herself. She was disconnected; I was unimpressed. But when my water broke and those contractions kicked in, I didn't give a damn who was wearing the catcher's mitt—I just wanted the baby O.U.T.

Still, when the nurse announced I'd dilated enough to push, like a fairytale princess riding in on the prettiest white stallion, Hilda waltzed into my labor and delivery room. You can't tell me there wasn't a soft white light shining down on her head as she made her way over to the bed, the most beautiful, relaxed smile on her face.

It was just after 2 a.m.

And with the assistance of a nurse whose name I didn't think to get, Hilda used her calm, soothing voice and her steady hands and her mighty powers to coax my Mari, my firstborn, the love of my life, out of my womb and, within 20 minutes of pushing, into my arms.

She may not recognize, remember, or think that what she did for me that night was all that special; goodness only knows how many babies Hilda Hutcherson delivered in her years as a well-respected, top ob-gyn in one of the busiest cities in the world. But I will never, ever forget Hilda—the kindness she showed me, the kindness she showed my body, the kindness she demanded I give myself by taking care of my health. And for sure, I'll never forget that she left her vacation and drove three hours in the middle of the night to help me receive the most precious Mother's Day gift this mom could ever receive: flesh of my flesh, blood of my blood—my beautiful baby girl.

Hilda stopped delivering babies shortly after Mari was born. I am so very grateful that she squeezed one more in before she changed her focus and took herself out of the delivery room.

For my baby's prenatal care, for my baby's safe passage into this world, Hilda, I simply say, God bless you. —*MAY 2011*

CHAPTER 2

Birthing While Black

T HERE ARE A TON OF THINGS I'll never forget about the first time I gave birth—showing up with a Donny Hathaway CD in one hand, a beautiful pink-and-white-striped "going home" dress and a white blanket handpicked special for my Mari in the other; being scared to death of the epidural needle but grateful that it smoothed me out almost immediately; waiting for what seemed like an eternity to see my baby's beautiful face; my ob-gyn and her deft, loving care of me and one of the loves of my life, my firstborn. Mari's baby soft skin against my breast—her breath as sweet as heaven.

But competing for my most memorable birthing moment is the not-so-special treatment I got that day. The hospital and workers where I had my first daughter sullied what should have been one of the most amazing days of my life.

I gave birth at a hospital in upper Manhattan—a renowned teaching hospital that, because of where it's situated, caters to a poor, uninsured community, but, because of its leading specialists, modern facilities, and state-of-the-art technology, also is frequented by well-to-do patients who consider it one of the best hospitals in New York. They made it very clear in the brochures and birthing plans that a regular ol' birth there was neither more nor less than what a pregnant women could get elsewhere, but if you were willing to fork over an additional $800 or so, you could get the Cadillac birthing experience: a private room, extra personal time with your significant other, a special waiting room for family members re-plete with free refreshments, and a complimentary congratulatory meal—two steak and lobster (!) dinners and champagne for two—for the new parents. I promise you this: the words were so pretty I was convinced I was about to give birth in a posh hotel.

I did not.

Despite an incredible birthing experience facilitated by my personal angel/ob-gyn, from almost the moment my baby took her first breath, her mother was treated like a 14-year-old drug-addicted welfare queen, there to push out yet another daddy-less baby. Seriously.

- They tested my newborn for drugs (though I've never taken an illicit substance in my entire life) without my consent—something I later found out hospitals do at disproportionately higher rates with black babies than white ones.
- Despite that I paid for the private room and meals, I was immediately put in a massive post-birth room with three other women and their newborns. I was moved only after I asked why I wasn't in a private room—a question that elicited scowls and foot-dragging from the nurse until she bothered to check my paperwork to see that, indeed, I'd paid for a private room. It took three hours for my room to be changed.
- Once in the private room, the nurses disappeared for nine hours! Seriously. *Nine.* I had no diapers. No idea how to breastfeed properly (and no bottle to feed my baby the formula they pushed on me in my new mom "goodie bag"). No instructions on what to do to care for my post-birth body (was it okay to walk? Pee? Wash?). Nothing. I seriously thought I was being punished for asking (nicely) for what I'd paid for. When a nurse finally

did show up, she came with a "gift bag" full of Similac and coupons for . . . Similac.

- The private "suite" was disgusting. The bathroom smelled like cheap, potent cleaning chemicals. The shower tiles were grimy and the shower curtain was full of mold. There wasn't so much as a picture on the bland walls. (I begged my backup ob-gyn to let me go home after one night; thank God, she signed off on it.)
- The nursing staff was genuinely surprised (!) that the guy by my side, Nick, was my husband—and actually said that stupid ish out loud.
- Our special meal arrived only after we pointed out to the nurses that the fees we paid included it, and by the time it got to us, our dinner was cold and our champagne (a tiny handheld bottle we could have finished with one big sip from the straw) was warm.

I couldn't get out of that place fast enough. And when it came time for me to have my second child, I stayed far, far away from that hospital—even changed my ob-gyn, which really broke my heart to do—to avoid it like the damn plague.

I wondered then what I know to be true now: It didn't matter how much money I had in my bank account or how good my insurance was, or that I had a ring on my finger, or that I was smart and accomplished, or that I tried to pay my way out of substandard service. At the end of the day, to almost everyone in that hospital, I was just another black girl pushing out another black baby and neither of us deserved to be treated with dignity or respect, much less specially. That human beings charged with caring for new life and the people who ushered in that miracle could traffic in this kind of reprehensible treatment of anyone, much less a new mother—no matter her race, financial or marital status, or background—is beyond my level of comprehension.

But it happens. A lot. And there are studies that show that my birthing experience is a lot like that of other African American women who've had babies in hospitals.

I bring up these things because the *New York Times* ran a story, "Chefs, Butlers, Marble Baths: Hospitals Vie for the Affluent," about how hospitals are creating special wings and services to attract and cater to the wealthy. The story, no doubt dreamed up in an editors' meeting after the whole debacle created after folk got wind of the opulent birthing suite and special treatment Beyoncé got when she gave birth to Blue Ivy Carter at Lenox Hill Hospital in 2012, kind of makes it seem like this is some kind of new phenomenon. I know better, though: VIP treatment for folk willing to pay for it is not new. Neither is disrespecting and giving subpar care to people whom those in charge or extending care think are not worthy of VIP treatment.

And if you look like I did when I gave birth to my baby girl— like an African American woman giving birth to a black baby— you are decidedly not a VIP. Unless, of course, you are Beyoncé. Then maybe you and your baby have a chance. This is, perhaps, the saddest of all. —*JANUARY 2012*

CHAPTER 3

Birthing Babies in Jim Crow South

I NEVER HAD THE HONOR of meeting my grandmother, my daddy's mama. She died sometime in 1945, in bed in her house in Virginia, just a few days, I'm told, after she gave birth to the last of her seven babies—in the same bed where she birthed them all. No one knows for sure what caused her death. She did have asthma, and so there is a theory that she suffered a horrific attack that stole her air. But snatches of stories gleaned over time reveal that she could have died from complications associated with childbirth.

My father was 10. He was there when his mother gave birth and there, too, when his mother took her last breath. She spoke to her boy, asked him to fetch her something, and when he returned, she was gone. Writing that part does not come easy to me. I am the mother of two girls—one who at the time of this writing is almost 10—and I couldn't imagine giving birth and then giving up the ghost while my children watched. The thought of the terror in my dad's heart—in his eyes . . . my God, these things hurt me so.

I am convinced of two things: my grandmother did not have to die, and chances are that my grandmother's story is not unique. She was a poor black woman in the South in the '40s, which meant that a cocktail of Jim Crow laws, inadequate medical services for the poor, and a lack of trained physicians willing to care for African Americans was just as lethal for her as whatever took her away from her family—a cocktail that most likely contributed to the infant and maternal mortality rates in her rural state.

It is this that I'm reminded of when I consider the history of "birthing while black" in our country. I know that we want to paint rosy pictures of wise grandmothers catching babies with their strong, beautiful, wrinkled hands while a room full of sisters and aunties and sisterfriends wipe the birth mom's brow and tell her everything is going to be all right. In my mind's eye, I see black fathers pacing outside in the dark—excited, worried, waiting for news. I see big potbellied cauldrons full to the top with water boiling and spitting on top of wood burning stoves—fresh white linens waiting to swaddle new life. I hear the babies cry—sweet, piercing. I imagine them rooting for breast and clutching pointer fingers and nuzzling under chins. Happy. Content. Ready to conquer.

But then I remember. I remember my grandmother. I remember Henrietta Lacks, the African American woman who, having died from cervical cancer and hellish, ineffectual gynecological care at the hands of a doctor who didn't seem to give a damn, had her ovarian cells stolen and used for science, without her knowledge or permission. And I remember countless other nameless, faceless but important black women who toiled and got pregnant and toiled and gave birth and toiled and raised babies without benefit of health and reproductive justice.

Today, black women are no longer in the backwoods, making a way out of no way, depending solely on those wise old wrinkled hands to usher in new life and complications to take away their air. There are hospitals and doctors who will see us now, and medicines and interventions that help to save our babies and our mothers, and trained midwives and doulas standing at the ready to help us—*I mean really help us*—in ways that the traditional medical establishment won't, even to this day.

I do wish my grandmother had benefit of these things. And I thank God that I did. —*MARCH 2013*

CHAPTER 4

Going It Alone

A GROUNDBREAKING SURVEY of African American mothers on their pregnancy and birth experiences reveals that black moms have little support before, during, and after birth—a void that may explain why African American babies are disproportionately underweight and suffer high infant mortality.

A first-of-its-kind survey of 245 black women in Oregon was conducted by the International Center for Traditional Childbearing (ICTC), with help from Portland State University, as part of the group's push to get the Oregon Health Authority to investigate how doulas can improve birth outcomes for women of color.

ICTC founder and director Shafia Monroe told TheSkanner .com that while there is a need for more research, the survey verifies what she sees and hears from black women in Oregon. "Many are in the public health care system, they don't have access to or support to take birthing classes or maintain breastfeeding, they often give birth alone with no support besides hospital staff, and some expressed fear during their time in the hospital based on their treatment," she added.

The study found that:

- Nearly two-thirds of the women surveyed did not attend birth education classes prior to delivery
- Nearly one-third of the women were concerned about their treatment during the birth of their baby

- The majority of women surveyed have government-paid health insurance coverage
- More than half of the women surveyed were single
- Only 25 percent of African American mothers were still breastfeeding their babies at six months, compared to more than 60 percent of Oregon moms overall. The national average is 40 percent.

The ICTC, an organization that promotes midwifery, recruitment, and training for black women interested in being doulas, says it's seen a marked improvement in birth outcomes for African American babies when black women have access to affordable, community-based, direct healthcare services like doulas. "A greater level of cultural competency is needed in order to ensure that basic trust and communication issues are not barriers to appropriate healthcare for black women and infants," Monroe added.

No truer words could have been said. I've written about how songstress Erykah Badu, who is studying for her midwifery license, partnered with the ICTC to help spread the word about the need for the healthcare community to think more deeply about the business of birth as it relates to African American mothers and especially its effects on black infant mortality rates. Thank God a group of passionate black women is leading the discussion. *taps mic* Is the health care community listening? —DECEMBER 2011

CHAPTER 5

My Super Weird Pregnancy Craving

S o I WAS DOING LAUNDRY and Mari came in and did what she's been doing since she was but a little pea in my womb: She shoved her face into the Tide bottle, inhaled deeply, and proclaimed her love for the scent of our favorite laundry detergent. Okay, well, she couldn't have possibly done that while in utero. But Lord knows that when I was pregnant, I couldn't walk past a laundry room without wanting to crunch on powdered Tide, liquid Downy, and all manner of cleaning product, especially Mr. Clean.

No, I never actually ate or sipped any. I might have inhaled deeply, but none actually touched my lips. Um, not really.

Of course, later in my pregnancy, I found out that my craving for powdered Tide was a symptom of an iron deficiency. But even as I swallowed those constipation-inducing horse er, iron pills, I knew deep down on the inside that it was my Mari who wanted to have a Tide pie. She proves me right every time I do laundry and especially when we walk down the laundry aisle at Kroger. Girlfriend's got it bad.

Anyway, yeah. Pregnancy cravings—and the babies who cause them—make us moms do the weirdest things. —*FEBRUARY 2011*

CHAPTER 6

The Baby Who Never Was

T HE CRAMPING STARTED IN THE CAR—sharp pains that felt like the spasms I get when my period is imminent. By the time I got back to our apartment and settled in from an afternoon of pedicures and massages at a spa party with my girlfriends, my groin felt like it was being shanked by 20 angry men. And the blood would not . . . stop . . . coming.

Hushed calls to Nick . . . rushed ride to the hospital . . . needles and pokes and questions from men in white coats . . . uncertainty. Tears. Fear. Maybe I had a cyst on my ovaries that burst. Maybe I had fibroids. Maybe it was a period more painful than usual, they said. An ER room full of physicians, but nobody knew what the problem was—just that I was in pain and bleeding and then suddenly not, and whatever "it" was, it was for my doctor to sort out, but it probably wasn't anything too major.

Turns out it was major.

"You had a miscarriage," my ob-gyn said easily—too easily. Like she was telling me, "Oh, by the way, you have sleep in your eye," or "There's lint on your shirt," or "Here's tissue—you have a booger." These things happen, she explained in measured, clipped, technical terms. You get pregnant and the embryo isn't sufficient and your body, knowing it's not sustainable, expels it.

I could barely process her words; the four most hurtful ones— *you, had, a,* and *miscarriage*—crackled like thunder over all the others, and the tears—oh, the tears—rushed from my eyes like the endless torrent of water down Niagara Falls.

"You'll be fine," she said. Insisted, really.

But I wasn't fine. I wasn't fine at all.

See, Nick and I had been trying to get pregnant for a few months before then—had gone through all the requisite paces to create a family together. I was a folic acid and vitamin-popping, temperature-checking, ovulation-stalking lunatic—doing everything the books said I needed to do to get pregnant. And my husband, bless his heart, came along for the ride, dutifully doing his part to make our dream of creating a little human being together a reality, even when it started feeling more like a chore than a loving act between a man and his wife.

And that month when my period was late and I peed on the stick and I saw the faint pink line, I wrinkled my brow and got kinda happy for the kinda news that the pregnancy test seemed to be telling me. Maybe I was pregnant. Maybe I wasn't. A faint line meant something, right? *Right?* I was going to be a mother. Maybe.

The blood test at my doctor's office confirmed that I was, indeed, pregnant. And then I was not. And for weeks, I mourned the baby that never was—this child who was supposed to have been my firstborn. I wondered if that baby was a girl who would have been round and sweet and chocolatey like me—or a rough-and-tumble thick little boy who would have been full of giggles and energy and spirit, with big ears like his daddy. Mostly, I wondered why God would see fit to let me get pregnant and, before I even knew for sure if I was with child, would take my baby away from here.

He blessed me with three others, though—two little girls I carried and birthed on my own, and a stepson, all of whom bring me joy every day. And I am grateful for every hour, every minute, every second that I have with them. But all these years later, I still wonder about the baby who never was. And I get a little angry that my doctor seemed a little too nonchalant about our loss. And a whole lot sad when I consider how many women have suffered miscarriages only to be hushed up. Only to have the devastation dismissed as a "natural" act. Only to be admonished for being shocked and then sad and then angry and forced to deal with the emotional trauma of it all alone.

Maybe things have changed since that fateful day when my baby was here and then not. Maybe doctors aren't as callous and clinical about something so hurtful and real for the whopping 20 percent of women whose pregnancies end in miscarriage. Maybe there are more places to find information now, rather than the paltry paragraphs I found picked over and buried deep in the few pregnancy books I could find in which the subject was even mentioned. More women certainly are speaking up about their experiences—rocker Pink revealed she got pregnant after suffering a miscarriage, and former president George Bush's revelation about his mother's miscarriage in his book opened up a short national conversation on the topic. Those spontaneous conversations do help women who've gone through it make it to the other side—out of the depression and darkness and into the comfort of knowing that they're not alone and there is still hope and options and life after the loss of a pregnancy. The loss of a child.

Still, people talk in hushed tones when the subject comes up or they cloak it in right-to-life vs. pro-choice arguments (for the record, though I do not believe abortion is right for me, I am staunchly pro-choice and believe with my whole heart that it is a woman's personal, individual right to decide for herself what she wants to do with her body), or, like they do with all too many women's health issues, miscarriage and the causes and study of it simply go ignored.

But for us mothers, the pain remains.

All these years later, I can attest to this.

I'm still missing my baby who never was. —*NOVEMBER 2010*

CHAPTER 7

Adoption and "The Blood": Embracing the True Meaning of Love, Family, and the Ties That Bind

I AM ADOPTED. It is not something that I choose to focus on or talk about much. Because for most of my life, it has meant nothing to me. Bettye and James Millner are my parents—they raised me, taught me, disciplined me, protected me. Love(d) me. This is all that has ever mattered.

Still, one day recently while we were making our way to a Saturday soccer game, we were listening to the "Strawberry Letter" segment on the *Steve Harvey Morning Show* when a listener intimated that her husband was against adoption because he didn't want someone else's "throwaway."

Throwaway.

That word stung. And it sat with me for the rest of the day, and through the weekend, clean into Monday. In the 30-plus years since I found my adoption papers, I've always thought of myself as the lucky one—the one that God saw fit to bless with a mother and father who chose me. Who wanted me. Who thought me worthy of their time and attention and love. Never once did it occur to me that there are people in this world who think of us adoptees as lesser-thans. Tainted.

Trash.

I mean, I've heard people insist that they want to make their "own" baby—a child who bears their "own" DNA. Who carries their blood. I get that, I guess. As an adoptee, it meant something to me to carry babies in my belly and push them through my loins and suckle them at my breast and search them from the tops of their curly little heads down to their tiny toes for evidence—signs of my blood, my DNA, my legacy in the only two people on the planet I know for sure are related by blood to me.

Still, it hurt me to the core to know, for sure, that there are people in this world who insist the love that I share with my parents is somehow less "legitimate" than that which I have for my own kids because my mom, dad, and I are not related by blood. And when I tell you it unhinged me, I mean, really, it unhinged me.

Until I got wind of my Mari's poem. It is a lovely piece she penned for a grade-wide competition in her junior high. I had no idea she'd written it, this piece she titled, "The Blood." It was at Parents Night that I first learned about it—that Mari's "The Blood" not only existed but also had won the competition over every other eighth-grade submission at the school and that it was to be presented in front of all the parents who'd ventured out to hear about our kids' school curriculum.

And when Mari's teacher read her poem, I cried. Like, an ugly, snotty cry. Because while I was letting some stupid letter from a radio show make me feel bad that I do not share my parents' blood, my then-13-year-old daughter was thinking about blood and its beauty in a deeper, more spiritual, powerful, and transcending way. Her words blew me away—made me remember that even in its distinction, blood is so much grander than its direct lines. That it is the glue that binds us all together—as one. The human race.

For your insight, Mari, I simply give thanks.

Here, I proudly present, "The Blood."

THE BLOOD
By MARI CHILES

The Blood.
The Blood that runs through my veins, my brain, my heart.

The blood, the biggest puzzle piece making me. And only me.
I cannot fathom how much blood.
The same blood that was running through my veins
    when I took my first breath.
When I made my first appearance, my first impression
    on my people. On this world.
I cannot fathom how much blood.
The same blood that is just one ripple, one little wave,
    one teaspoon, in the sea of blood.
The gallons and gallons of heritage.
The big body of being, with everyone's little ripples and
    little waves and little teaspoons coursing through it.
Until millions of different families become one.
I cannot fathom how little blood.
But my little teaspoon carries the world.
My blood flows back to Somalia and Ethiopia hundreds
    and hundreds of years ago.
My blood flows back to my slave ancestors.
My blood flows through everything, everyone.
People interconnect and reconnect.
Blood flows and mixes together.
And we know that we are the same.
That is how the beautiful blood works.
The Blood.
The blood of generations that found its way into your veins.
It is golden.
All of that blood.
It trickles down to you.
That little teaspoon
In the body of being.

—OCTOBER 2012

NEW MOTHERHOOD

CHAPTER 8

Nipples and Ninny

IT WAS A NO-BRAINER FOR ME: All the books said I should breastfeed my baby because it was best for her and that she would be stronger, faster, smarter, better for it. And so I rushed out and bought myself a fancy Medela breast pump and stocked up on breast milk storage bags and got all giddy when I started filling out my nursing bras. (Um, yeah I was the president of the Itty Bitty Titty Committee and so the prospect of having boobies was a huge plus on my Reasons Why I Should Breastfeed list.) And I proudly told anyone who would listen that I planned to feed my child the natural way—the way my mother's generation and all the generations before hers did, too. The way God intended.

Um, yeah. The nurses at the hospital where I gave birth to my beautiful Mari had other intentions. I mean, in theory, breastfeeding made all the sense in the world for me and my baby. But in the real world, a.k.a. a hospital in the middle of Harlem, where the environment made doctors and staff more prone to assume that a young black woman pushing out a baby was single, poor, uneducated, and alone, breastfeeding just didn't fit into the equation.

And so the nurse put my Mari in my arms and disappeared, leaving me for nine hours with nothing more than my baby and a goodie bag full of coupons for baby lotion and soap, useless pamphlets, and two packages of baby formula. I was absolutely terrified, overwhelmed, exhausted, and clueless; I simply didn't know how to feed my newborn child. No manner of picture/

conversation/book chapter prepared me for The Show—the actual breastfeeding of my baby. Was I supposed to be sitting any particular way? Pop in my boob any kind of way? Squeeze it to help get the milk into her mouth? Where was the milk anyway?

I mean, I was convinced the baby would starve to death. And that she would die with a piece of my nipple in her mouth (those little gums were killer, especially when I unwittingly pulled my breast out of her mouth).

When a nurse finally made her way back into my room, she seemed surprised to find me breastfeeding. (She was also surprised that I had a husband, insurance, a good job, and that Mari was my first child, as discussed in the "Birthing While Black" essay on page 10.) Still, she made quick work of showing me how to get the baby to latch on, how to get her to stop sucking, and, most importantly, she gave me a number to La Leche League so that I could ask an expert questions on how to feed my baby the right way.

Getting the breastfeeding right wasn't easy or natural; for the first two weeks, the skin on my nipple was literally shredded and my breasts were raw; it was like a toothless little man was sucking on an open, achy wound. I'd smooth Lansinoh on my skin between feedings and sit shirtless with ice packs on my nipples, and literally cry out when Mari latched on.

But I didn't give up.

Through the pain.

Through the doubts.

Through the pumping in the bathroom at work.

Through the ridicule from my more old-school friends and family members who wondered loudly and unabashedly when I'd stop letting my baby suck on my ninny.

I breastfed my baby for 10 months, and pumped and fed her my milk for 2 more months after that, even after she stopped taking my breast. I was proud of myself for hanging in there. And proud of my daughter, too, for being patient with me. I know that it would have been just as easy for her to reject my breast. But she didn't. And for this, I'm grateful.

There are plenty of moms who aren't as fortunate—who don't have the benefit of expensive breast pumps and copious amounts of time to recuperate from the painful beginning stages of breast-feeding or halfway understanding bosses who give them time to pump or even a pamphlet's worth of information telling them how it's done or extolling its benefits. These are things that some of us breastfeeding moms simply take for granted.

Of course, there are plenty of moms who forgo breastfeeding to formula feed and this is their right. No judgment here. To each her own.

But I thank goodness that there are plenty of resources available for moms who do want to successfully breastfeed, much more than was available when I had Mari back in the late '90s.

And for this, we should all be grateful. —*OCTOBER 2009*

CHAPTER 9

Cry It Out: The Method That Kills Baby Brain Cells

I KNOW. A DRAMATIC HEADLINE. Made you look. But it's not fiction. It turns out that the "Cry It Out" method of baby sleep training, where you ignore that your kid is screaming, crying, and turning 40 shades of purple so that she can break herself out of the habit of being spoiled and cuddled to sleep, does more harm—way more—than good.

In piece for *Psychology Today*, Darcia Narvaez, an associate professor of psychology at Notre Dame, writes that when babies are stressed, their bodies release cortisol into their systems—a toxic hormone that kills brain cells. Considering their brains are only 25 percent developed when they're born full-term and grow rapidly in their first year, killing off baby brain cells is a huge *no bueno*. Narvaez notes that studies out of Harvard, Yale, Baylor, and other prestigious institutions show that said killing off of baby brain cells can lead to the higher probability of ADHD, poor academic performance and anti-social tendencies, and that human babies are hardwired for hands-on comfort and care.

"Babies are built to expect the equivalent of an 'external womb' after birth . . . being held constantly, breastfed on demand, needs met quickly," Narvaez writes. "These practices are known to facilitate good brain and body development. When babies display discomfort, it signals that a need is not getting met, a need of their rapidly growing systems."

Um, remember that scene from the "True Hollywood Stories: Rick James" episode on *Chapelle's Show*—the one where Rick James is grinding his feet into Eddie Murphy's couch? Yeah. *insert an image of Denene doing the Rick James foot stomp into the couch thing here* In your face, Nick Chiles! For the record, I argued and fussed and fought with my husband over "Ferberizing" our Mari. The infant self-soothing technique, invented by Dr. Richard Ferber, requires parents to let their babies cry it out for a predetermined amount of time, in increasing intervals, before they comfort them—and even then, comforting involves talking to and rubbing the babies; picking them up or cuddling them is forbidden.

Now, it's been well over a decade and a half since we tried this cry it out thing with Mari, but I promise you, I can still hear her screaming in her crib in the next room. My breasts would throb at her every whimper, and every second on the clock would feel like an eternity while I waited for my chance to go in and pat her on her stomach, rub her arm and cheek and tell her, "It's okay, baby—Daddy promises you won't die from crying."

But I was. It just didn't feel right to let my child scream and holler and thrash by her little self in the dark in her crib when I knew full well that a little rocking in her glider, maybe a song and a sweet nuzzle of her cheek would send her off to dreamland. Granted, some nights that meant multiple rocking/singing/nuzzle times, but, to me, it was a small price to pay for feeling like I was mothering my baby and helping her feel like her mommy was there. Always there.

Of course, plenty of other parents think differently about it and that's their right. We all do what we think works for our kids, our families, our lives. Not gonna point fingers at y'all. But I will point them at the hubs. When I showed him stories chronicling Narvaez's anti-cry-it-out research—and an interview in which Ferber actually backs off his own method—Nick shrugged his shoulders and said, "It ain't fun for the baby, but that shit worked. Everybody got some sleep. You going for two years with only three hours of sleep at night isn't healthy either."

I think he might have said those exact words to me the first time I left Mari in her crib. Still, as much as his reasoning made sense, it just didn't feel right to me—her mother. And when Nick told Mari we did this to her when she was a baby, she was incredulous: "What? You used to let me cry? You didn't come get me? *You just left me there by myself?!*"

That was Daddy, baby!

Yeah. That Ferber training didn't last long in our house, and I don't remember even trying it with my Lila. (Which might explain why our daughters' nighttime routines were a little worthy-of-a-Broadway-production hectic for longer than they should have been. But whatevs.) My babies and I benefited greatly from our nightly bonding sessions and co-sleeping arrangements, and I'm glad I did it for as long as I did.

Now that we've got this babies-need-to-cry-it-out business out of the way, I've got some ideas on what researchers need to look into next: I'm waiting for the study to show that beating your kid like she stole something in what is supposed to be a friendly game of Go Fish or Checkers causes brain melt. I'm looking at you, Nicholas Chiles. I'm looking at you. —*DECEMBER 2011*

CHAPTER 10

Photos of Celebrity Post-Baby Bodies Suck for Making Us Feel Craptastic about Our Baby Weight

Y EARS AGO when she had a new album out and was still in love with Jermaine Dupri and her brother Michael was still in the land of the living, I interviewed Janet Jackson for a feature story in *Essence*. On stage and in magazines, she's an absolute glamour doll, but let me tell you this: in person, Janet, sans the stage makeup, perfectly coiffed hair and uber sexy, body-skimming costume, is breathtakingly stunning, with a body that makes you want to quit food, eat air, buy lifetime stock in Spanx and spend every waking moment in somebody's gym.

But by the second day of our interview—this time at her posh apartment overlooking Central Park—I confirmed what I'd always suspected about Janet and other celebrities famous not just for their talent but their beautiful bodies: they look the way they do—"perfect"—because they pay people to keep them that way. Sure, celebrities have to have some level of commitment in watching what they eat and exercising, but Janet admitted that she hated working out and employed a full-time trainer whose sole job it was to literally drag her out of bed and make her exercise. She acknowledged, too, that she had a nutritionist and chef on hand to design and prepare all her meals and snacks—a revelation punctuated by a dude who was on hand to personally give her milkshakes and vitamins practically every hour during our two-day interview.

Of course, most celebrities stay fit and thin because their jobs demand it and they want to stay off *National Enquirer*'s weekly "Celebrity Cellulite: Whose Flabby Ass Is This?" cover stories. But we mere mortals often aren't privy and have no access to the tricks and help celebrities employ to keep themselves slim and beautiful.

Which is why I'm always *highly* annoyed by the "how they lost the weight" stories that show celebrity moms two seconds after they dropped their babies posted up practically naked on magazine covers, looking like they didn't just carry and push a human from their loins. The inference always seems to be, "Take note you fat, sloppy mothers in your mom jeans, beat up sneakers and baby food-stained sweatshirts: real moms look hot after giving birth, and they do it effortlessly." Which of course makes me want to kick the celebrities and the dumb editors who push those stories dead in the back.

I say these things because the Internet once was abuzz with a most scintillating piece of journalism—an *Us Weekly* cover story of Mariah Carey in hot pants, stilettos, and a half shirt, with a headline screaming in neon yellow, "30 lbs in 3 Months! I Got My Body Back." Of course, the story wouldn't be complete without a super sad-looking "before" picture of Mariah pregnant with twins—as if carrying two babies in her stomach and enough milk in her breasts to feed them was just downright slovenly of her. For kicks and giggles, they added, "Mariah's easy day-by-day plan that you can do, too"—you know, so you can appear to be a hot MILF like Mariah. Oh—and don't forget to go out there and get on that Jenny Craig. (Mariah was a spokeswoman. Surprise!)

And hot on the heels of the Mariah story was news that a very pregnant Jessica Simpson inked a $3 million deal with Weight Watchers to hit the treadmill as soon as she got off the maternity ward. That would be the same Jessica Simpson who spent the last few years fighting back against Hollywood for making fun of her curves and even created a short-lived show, *The Price of Beauty*, to show that the definition of beauty is different all across the world and shouldn't be dictated by a couple of movie producers and magazine editors in Hollywood. With Jessica's crossing over to the dark side, one could almost hear editors salivating while plotting magazine covers about how she'd lost all the weight and never felt better, and a book detailing her step-by-step guide to losing the mommy weight.

Yeah.

Raise a church finger and give an "amen" if you're tired of post-pregnant celebrity moms/diet company spokeswomen and the gossip wags that stalk them doing those tired "before and after" pregnancy weight stories. Really, they do nothing more than work overtime to convince new moms they suck because they carried a human in their stomachs for nine months and couldn't lose the baby weight before the first post-pregnancy checkup. Like, how many moms are pressuring themselves to eat unhealthy and strain their bodies with unreasonable workouts so they can be "hot" like the Hollywood moms plastering the magazine rack at the grocery store checkout?

I promise you, with all the things moms juggle when a new baby is added into the mix, the last thing we need is the TV, magazines, newspapers, and blogs screaming at us to look "effortlessly hot" two seconds after we drop our precious loads. Or a celebrity blog or book (Hello, Kourtney Kardashian!) finger-wagging at regular moms who don't have nannies damn near wet-nursing their children while some dude pulls them out of bed for exercise and shoves health shakes and gourmet meals in their faces at every turn.

I may not be a size two and I may still be carrying the residuals of my last pregnancy on my body here and there (yeah, I know I had my last baby almost two decades ago . . . so what's your point?!), but dammit, I look good.

And so do you, and you, and you, too. Kiss your pouch, touch those stretch marks, admire those not-so-perky-anymore breasts and those wide birthing hips and thick thighs and thank God for each of these things. After all, together they worked a miracle— gave you the power to create, produce, and sustain the most precious gift of all: human life.

Now somebody put *that* on the cover of a magazine.

—*DECEMBER 2011*

CHAPTER 11

Remembering the Newborn-in-Public Jitters

I CAN'T EXPLAIN WHY, but pictures of Beyoncé and Jay-Z taking their then-seven-week-old, Blue Ivy Carter, out on a lunchtime stroll in New York City for the first time dug up all kinds of crazy memories of me hoarding my then-newborn, Mari, in our apartment—too afraid to let anyone so much as breathe anywhere near her, let alone take her out in public.

I promise you: save for her visits to the pediatrician, my Mari didn't take in fresh air until well into July—more than six weeks after she came onto this earth on a cool early June morning, tiny, precious, vulnerable. Every book I'd read and our pediatrician, too, said we didn't need to sequester our daughter in the house—that there was no medical reason to avoid taking her outside. But that didn't stop my worst-case scenarios from taking over whenever I considered putting my baby in her stroller and crossing our apartment door threshold. What if the chill gives her a horrible cold and she dies? What if one of the ducks or dogs at the local park has fleas and it gets on the baby and she dies? What if a grubby little toddler sneezes on her or, worse, Dave the Dope Fiend Shooting Dope Who Don't Know the Meaning Of Water Nor Soap is lingering in the parking lot and he goes "blah!" in my baby's face and she dies?

Nope—I wasn't taking any chances.

Nobody was allowed in the house, save for my parents, Nick's parents, and our siblings—and every last one of them had to practically strip at the door, do the surgical scrub in the bathroom, and wear a layer of freshly washed cloth diapers on their shoulders and over their arms before they were allowed to pick up my baby.

Yup. I was *that* mom.

And if you think that was bad, you should have been there the first day I actually did take my baby for her first walk. It was at the park right next door to where we lived—no more than 15 paces from the back door of our apartment building. It was 80-something degrees outside. I wrapped that baby in a onesie, pants, a sweater, and a blanket, and stuffed a second blanket in a diaper bag filled with a half a box of diapers, a new packet of wipes, a bunch of diaper cloths, a change of clothes, a chest-full of baby toys, and three pacifiers. Just in case.

My God, I crack up now thinking about just how maniacal I must have seemed—like I was the first woman on the planet to ever have a baby. But isn't that how we do with the first child? Exhausted, strung out and clueless, we stumble through our first weeks with our babies, damn-near memorizing every line in our stacks of baby books, Googling every little doggone burp/squeak/spit-up/poop/pee/cry, and tearily demanding the pediatrician call us right now, right now, *right now!* or else she can just meet us at the emergency room. Basically, driving ourselves insane over our little miracles.

Of course, my poor Lila, who came three years later, didn't get the "benefit" of a clueless mommy. By then, I was a know-it-all. She was lucky if I bothered to wipe off her pacifier when it hit the floor. She'd live. And be just fine. Come to think of it, this is probably why the little one is so doggone tough. Strong. There was no babying that kid. It was what it was. Is what it is.

Anyway, more power to Beyoncé and Jay-Z for getting little Blue Ivy out of their apartment and out into the beautiful streets of New York City for her first stroll around town. I can only imagine the anxiety the singer faced wrapping her baby up in a bundle of leopard print cloth and all manner of blankets to shield her baby not just from the winter chill but the prying eyes of paparazzi, fans, and haters who continued to question her, her husband, and their beautiful, young family. Probably helps to have a 7-foot, 300-pound bodyguard moving lockstep with you, but still, good for them. —*FEBRUARY 2012*

CHAPTER 12

Advice for Dealing with Baby No. 2, from a Mom Who's Been There

B EFORE I HIP YOU to the second baby game, I need my second baby, my little Lila, to know this one true thing: she was wanted, made from love and the product of lots of plotting and planning and prayer—truly a gift from God.

That said: Girl, get ready. First babies are sweet and sugary and all kinds of good, but Sweet Baby Jesus in the Manger: second babies are no joke. I got pregnant with my Lila two years after my Mari was born, just days before September 11. Already exhausted by being a mom to a toddler, a wife in a relatively young marriage, a full-time working mom, and an author and freelancer in the little bit of spare time that I had, moving with a baby in my belly was . . . difficult. Yes, that's what I'll call it: difficult. Even though I knew what to expect, so many things were different with Lila: whereas I was young and energetic during most of my first pregnancy, my second just made me feel worn out—stressed, tired, fat. Concerned, especially, how I was going to balance it all.

Nobody warned me. And all that free and unsolicited advice I got with the first pregnancy? Yeah, nobody could be bothered with my second.

And so if it is, indeed, true that you're pregnant with your second, there are some things you're going to have to get ready for. To know. No lie.

I got you girl.

Here, Top 20 Things I Want You to Know about Becoming a Second-Time Mom:

1. Remember when nobody could tell you were pregnant until you were damn near heading into the third trimester? Right. Say hello to the "belly pop" at about three months.

2. Oh, and say goodbye, too, to your ankles, that cute pregnancy glow, and any semblance of energy. You were super cute pregnant the first time just because. The second time? *Right.*

3. Cuddling the toddler while the other baby is wrapping toes around your ribs and pressing on your lady parts is . . . interesting.

4. So is trying to convince *Numero Uno* that she should be totally cool that she's about to be dethroned. Don't expect Firstborn to play nice. Start prepping her with the "being a big sister is awesome" spiel now to help avert the new baby sibling choke-out later.

5. Don't make any plans for that second baby shower. You'll be lucky if Grandma and your sister come up off a gift.

6. When the baby is born, you'll go through diapers a little more sparingly. As in, "really, she won't die if she pees in that one a second time."

7. Same goes for germs. Let's just say the "Five Second Rule" for Firstborn's pacifiers morphs easily into the, "I Know It Fell Underneath the Refrigerator and the Dog Licked It, but the Baby Will Be Just Fine Rule" for Baby No. 2. It is what it is, kid. Think of it as an awesome boost for the immune system. Yup! *in my Jay-Z voice*

8. *Doc McStuffins* marathon? Heck yeah. How else is an exhausted mom of two supposed to get some rest?

9. No, babies aren't supposed to watch R-rated movies and yes they should be sleeping in their own beds at a decent hour, but if Jimmy Fallon and The Roots aren't knocking around, you're totally good.

10. Remember when you swore the "Cry It Out" method would be the death of you and your baby? Uh huh. Second baby +

a few teary nights = sane mommy + trained baby who goes the eff to sleep.

11. Hand-me-downs are awwwwesome! Especially if the babies are the same sex.

12. You'll potty train like a champ, yo.

13. But your poor kid is going to come up really short on those baby pictures. And special songs written off full hearts, fresh out of the labor and delivery room. Pro tip: tell the new baby the camera was broken. And daddy couldn't get studio time. Or something.

14. Don't worry about that second-baby baby weight. We all get it. And keep it.

15. Mommy/Daddy sexy time? Uh huh. I hope you got some real fond memories of those pre-baby days, circa "Crazy in Love."

16. Thumbs up to the two-baby booty, though.

17. Triple the amount of time it takes to get out the door. Triple that if you're having another girl.

18. Meeting the physical and emotional needs of two kids at the same damn time will feel like you're trying to guard LeBron James and Dwyane Wade by your damn. Know that you cannot win. But eventually, they'll know and respect that you tried. Maybe.

19. Know, too, that the first baby will be her daddy's project over the next few years; keeping the first one happy, occupied, and sane becomes his top priority while you tag team with the little one.

20. You'll be fine in no time. So will your man and your babies. No matter how crazed you feel, looking into those two sweet faces will erase every . . . single . . . bit . . . of . . . tomfoolery that comes with raising two kids. Pinky swear. —*MAY 2013*

CHAPTER 13

Black & Proud: Tending To the Self-Esteem of Black Children

I T'S A RITUAL I BEGAN the first day my girlpie, Mari, started kindergarten. I'd fluff her super cutie outfit, adjust the fancy barrettes in her hair, take her little moon pie face into my hands, kiss those beautiful cinnamon brown cheeks, and pump her up all the way from the garage to the front steps of her school, where she was the only black girl in her class. "You are fantastic, baby girl—the smartest little girl I know," I'd say, looking directly into her big browns, like a trainer does a sweaty heavyweight champ between rounds in a boxing bout. "Be fabulous, because who are you not to be?"

Kids who hear they're the best tend to believe it and rise to the challenge—particularly black children. A study published in the journal *Child Development* backs me up on this; the study, authored by Ming-Te Wang, assistant professor of psychology in education at the University of Pittsburgh, and James P. Huguley of Harvard University, found that when parents promote feelings of racial knowledge, pride, and connection, black kids do better in school.

Mr. Wang and Mr. Huguley could have saved themselves some time and research cash; those of us black parents in the know would have happily told this to them quickly and for free.

Affirmations chased Mari and my baby girl, Lila, into classrooms in New Jersey and Georgia for years—encouragement I thought important enough to repeat again and again. For the sake of my daughters. For the sake of their psyches and their self-esteem. For their own good.

They wear the armor.

It's a brilliant coat of self-confidence instilled in them since the womb, not only because I believe them to be clever and beautiful, but because the world conspires to tell my girls different—to ingrain in their brains that something is wrong with their kinky hair and their juicy lips and their dark skin and their piercing brown eyes and their bubble butts and thick thighs and their beautiful brains and their eclectic culture and black girl goodness. I promise you, some days—a lot of days—it feels like I'm guarding them from a tsunami of "you're ugly/dumb/fat/incompetent/inadequate/insert-your-racial-insult-here" pronouncements; magazines and TV shows and popular radio and movies and all of the rest of pop culture act as if black girls, teens, and women do not exist on most days, and on the extra special ones, we are reduced to hypersexualized, drink-tossing, weave-pulling stripper bullies, climbing our way to the top on the backs of rappers and ballers.

Then there are the micro-aggressions that feel like death by a million cuts: the teachers who assume my girls are below average, until they discover quite the contrary; the store clerks who follow us—even the 10-year-old—around the store, until we pull out the cash at the register; the silly mothers who practice their "hey, girlfriend!" theater around us, until they find out the hard way that we don't do Ebonics in mixed company.

Don't believe me? Spend a little time on children's channels; my daughters can go, literally, for hours without seeing anyone who looks like them. Then flip over to MTV, VH1, Oxygen, and all the other homes of "reality" shows (or any show that's not written and produced by TV "It" girls Shonda Rhimes or Ava DuVernay, both African American women with hit shows), and watch the necks swizzle and the weaves fly. Come with us to the mall on a quiet Tuesday afternoon. Or to a school mom gathering.

I can't have my daughters thinking they are invisible. Or worse, that they're ignorant, loud caricatures unworthy of respect. So I make a point of encouraging my girls to own their beauty—on the inside and out. And I demand that they pull and stretch and reach for the highest rung, because they're capable of being more talented, brilliant, and confident than any other kid who crosses their paths, black or white—in the classroom, on the soccer field, on the stage, in all that they do.

Examples of black folks who've achieved this abound: I surround my daughters with books by and about people of color who've shined a light on the beauty and complexity of us—fill their ears with the music of masters who rep us with their talent and lyricism. Television and movies are watched with a critical eye; our complicated history is explored and talked about and picked through—our culture celebrated through food and travel and relationships. They are told "we are an amazing people" loudly and often, not just during Black History Month or Martin Luther King, Jr.'s birthday, but every day.

And most importantly, my daughters are made to understand and know that 24 hours a day, 7 days a week, 365 days of the year, they are expected to bring home the top grades in their classes. No exception. I'm not all Tiger Mom about it mind you, just a huge cheerleader and a no-nonsense support system who works hard with my girls to make them understand their true potential.

After all, when a child is told that she is fearfully and wonderfully made, who is she *not* to be fabulous? —JANUARY 2013

CHAPTER 14

For Black Children Who Color Outside the Lines

ABOUT THIS, I'm really clear: if Lila, my littlest one, were left to her own devices (and her parents had more time, cash, connections, and people), she'd be off somewhere fancy, ordering up room service, sipping a Sprite with lime, twirling about in her favorite sparkly black and hot pink Twinkle Toes sneakers and a wild, flashy dress that would make Lady Gaga look demure, talking 'bout, "Can somebody turn my mic up high when I hit the stage, Mommy?"

Yes, Lila is *that* kid.

Full of spirit—wild and free.

Oh, trust: Nick and I have tried just about every disciplinary tool we could think of to tame that kid, but she remains thoroughly unbroken. Shoot, she isn't even bent. And on our good days, we admit to a certain amount of grudging admiration for her strength of will and busy ourselves with an deep curiosity about what this child will grow up to be. The fact of the matter is that she is who she is and, tempted as we may be to want her to tamp down the 500-watt sparkle and shine, we're working really hard to let our babies—even, and especially, the wild one—be exactly who they are.

This is a new concept around my way because my parents' generation and the generations of African Americans who came before ruled their homes with iron fists; thick, fresh, prickly switches; and The Code: Children are to walk the line—to be seen, not heard. Coloring outside the lines—whether it be the way we dress, talk, act, or just are—was a huge *no bueno*.

Which, I guess, worked for our parents. But not always for us. I'm passionate about instilling confidence in my kids and write about it often, simply because I know firsthand what being forced to color inside the lines can do to a girl's self-esteem—how being quiet and tragically deferential and afraid to express one's self out of an abiding belief that you have no right to speak up can get you walked on. Makes you miss out on your blessings.

On what you could be.

It was this I was thinking about when the e-streets were clucking about Willow Smith, daughter of Hollywood power couple Will and Jada, becoming a pop star. At the tender age of nine, she became an overnight rap/singing sensation when her new single, "Whip," became a viral smash, getting more than 100,000 hits in the first day of release on the YouTube yard. Shortly after, rapper/producer/world dominator Jay-Z signed li'l Ms. Smith to a recording deal with his Roc Nation label and compared her to a young Michael Jackson.

Willow was following in the footsteps of her brother, Jaden, who got an early jump on his career when he made his film debut in *The Pursuit of Happyness*—at the tender age of eight.

And, in typical fashion, folks were all over the Internet, bashing the song, questioning Will and Jada's judgment as parents, breaking on Jay-Z for signing a nine-year-old to a record label that boasts provocative rappers, launching mean-spirited comments about the girl's shaved hair and clothing choices. I mean, you'da thunk the girl knocked back a fifth of bourbon for breakfast, ate small children for lunch, and then strolled the red carpet with Satan.

Like, come on, folks: Willow Smith is the child of a rapper-turned-actor who is, perhaps, one of the most well-respected, famous, and loved performers of his generation. His wife is no slouch in front of the camera, either, and their son became an official international heartthrob in his own right after his star turn in the *Karate Kid* remake. The Smith family entertains. And it does it well. And a huge part of the world the Smiths live in has an obvious belief that you let your kids express themselves—that you don't stifle their creativity. Isn't it only natural, then, that Willow wants to follow in those footsteps? And that her parents oblige her by letting her be exactly who she is—shaved hair, shades, glitter, animal print knee-high boots, microphone, rap career and all?

I won't even get into the sexism of it all—how nobody had a problem when the Smiths let Jaden become a child actor and wear his hair wild and woolly and be exactly who he wanted to be. That's for another post. No, this post is about how Will and Jada's decision to let their daughter be who she is—full of spirit and wild and free—smacks up against the conventional wisdom of black America that children—especially girl children—are to live by The Code: Sit back. Be quiet. Play the rear. And always—always!—color within the lines.

I'd like to remind the naysayers that, had Jay-Z's mom not given him a boom box to encourage his love of music, he may not have grown up to be one of America's most successful artists and entrepreneurs. If someone had taken the violin out of Esperanza Spalding's hands when she was six, we would have never heard this virtuoso's incredible gift to modern-day jazz. What if Picasso hadn't picked up that paintbrush? What if Tracy Reese never felt the whiz of a sewing machine beneath her feet? Or Quincy Jones never saw Michael Jackson spin on his toes and sing James Brown's "I Got the Feelin'" with all his might?

What if your parents had just encouraged you to pursue your passion—no matter what everyone else had to say about it, no matter how outside of the "norm" it was?

I'm not suggesting things will be perfect for this child. The road to Hollywood is littered with the bodies of child stars who couldn't handle the success, money, and fame, and had quite a time making the hard transition from kid darling to adult zero. And if what happened to actor Laurence Fishburne's daughter when she announced she wanted to become famous by making adult sex movies is any indication, there's no great guarantee that keeping your child from rocking a Mohawk at age nine will keep her from spreading her legs for the camera at nineteen (side-eye at Montana Fishburne and her burgeoning porn career, Lindsay Lohan and her various drug- and alcohol-fueled penitentiary stints, and Kim Kardashian for just being *that* chick). But there's no evidence that allowing Willow Smith to be creative as a youngster is the first step down the road to drug- and alcohol-abusing, loudmouthed, overexposed hooker hell.

Nope, something tells me that Will and Jada won't have a problem keeping top eye out for their baby girl—won't hesitate to send her butt on home if it doesn't look/smell/feel right for their kid. Of course, I don't have any kind of evidence to support or back me up on their parental abilities—just a bunch of glittery, shiny pictures of their beautiful family, intact and in love, paving a new way for the rest of us mere mortals trying to parent our kids with a little bit more savvy than the parenting generations before us.

And this is what we all aspire to, isn't it? To be better than our parents? To raise happy, creative, aggressive, unafraid, bold, smart, interesting children who see what they want and just, like, go for it? While everyone else shakes their heads and demands that child sit down, I'll be over here, cheering on Willow being— and her parents for letting their daughter be—exactly who she is.

Who she wants to be.

My kid draws pictures of horses on her notebook, slays them on the soccer field, fancies herself a flutist, and wears Statue of Liberty outfits to the dinner table just because. Willow Smith shaves her hair and raps. By 14, both of them—my Lila and their Willow—will be on to new passions, forging new frontiers. Happy where they feel they belong. And coloring outside the lines. And we parents, if we're worth our salt, will be right there with them, cheering them on and providing the safety net they need as they find their way down their own paths. Doing our jobs.

So dance your dance, Lila.

And sing your song, Willow.

Whip your hair and *sang it.* —*MAY 2014*

CHAPTER 15

The Attack against Black Girl Beauty

I RUSHED OUT and bought a bunch of beautiful dresses and frilly booties and flouncy hats the second I found out my Mari was a girl. No, seriously: My first and second stops after the ultrasound were to Space Kiddets, a New York City boutique with an incredible collection of European children's wear, and ABC Carpet & Home, where they used to have this absolutely glorious children's boutique down in the basement full of pretty little things for pretty little girls. I swear, I literally skipped down the streets of lower Manhattan while I burned a hot hole in my purse buying clothes to fill my yet-to-be-born baby's closet.

Her wardrobe was to die for—a gorgeous collection for what I was confident was going to be a stunning little girl.

And like any mother who tucks her new baby girl into her first lovely dress, I looked at Mari's face and stared into her eyes and pulled her chubby little cheeks to mine and marveled at how striking she was.

And every morning, still, I do the same with both my girls. Some days, they'll just be talking to me about nothing in particular and I'll look up and catch a glimpse of Lila's big ol' almond eyes and that Hershey's Special Dark Chocolate-colored skin of hers, or Mari's perfect apple face and that ancient Egyptian nose, looking like it was carved to match the Sphinx, and it literally takes my breath away.

They are, simply, beautiful girls.

I tell them this often.

Not just because I believe it to the core, but because the world conspires to tell my babies different—to ingrain in their brains that something is wrong with their kinky hair and their juicy lips and their dark skin and their piercing brown eyes and their bubble butts and thick thighs and black girl goodness. I promise you, it feels like I'm guarding them from a tsunami of "you're ugly" pronouncements; magazines and TV shows and popular radio and movies and all of the rest of pop culture insist on squeezing all of us women into a ridiculously Eurocentric, blonde-haired, light-eyed standard of beauty, but good God, unless you're parenting a little black girl, you have absolutely no earthly idea how exhausting it is to be media whipped for not being a white girl. I mean, for all the cocky, I-love-me-exactly-the-way-I-am declarations we black women make, some days, I wonder why we are not hurling our collective bodies off the side of Mount Kilimanjaro and just ending it all.

For sure, I was waving the white flag in surrender when I saw this madness shoot like wildfire across my favorite social media haunts: "Why Are Black Women Less Physically Attractive Than Other Women?" It's an article written by a researcher who thought it important enough to figure out who's prettiest, and approved by *Psychology Today*, a reputable scientific media outlet that found the researcher's arguments worth posting. For the sake of showing you just how utterly ridiculous and disgusting the researcher's study was, I will quote the most offensive piece of reasoning he used to deduce why black women are the ugliest of any race of people on the planet:

> The only thing I can think of that might potentially explain the lower average level of physical attractiveness among black women is testosterone. Africans on average have higher levels of

testosterone than other races, and testosterone, being an androgen (male hormone), affects the physical attractiveness of men and women differently. Men with higher levels of testosterone have more masculine features and are therefore more physically attractive. In contrast, women with higher levels of testosterone also have more masculine features and are therefore less physically attractive. The race differences in the level of testosterone can therefore potentially explain why black women are less physically attractive than women of other races, while (net of intelligence) black men are more physically attractive than men of other races.

Translation: My babies, beautiful as they are, will grow up to look like ugly, manly she-girls who, having nowhere near what it takes to have a man find her attractive enough to forge any kind of meaningful relationship, will die alone in their studio apartments in the hood, trails of dried butter pecan Häagen-Dazs dribbling down the corners of their mouths, surrounded by a bunch of cats, with old *Meet The Browns* reruns blaring from their tiny TVs. Surely, at their funerals, there will be no men to speak of; their ugliness will be far too much to bear for any man to want to be bothered to attend.

No, the study didn't go all the way *there*. But dammit, that's how it read to me, a black woman raising two black daughters—like someone had lifted excerpts from a Klan pamphlet, slapped some scientific research on top of it, parked it on a reputable site, and masqueraded it as stone cold fact.

To me, the study harkened back to the era of eugenics, when it was the order of the day to find some bogus scientific validation for the kind of biases passed on to people by their parents and their communities when folk grasped for anything to try to justify their bigotry and hatred. I'm not naive enough to think we're past bias in our global community; what we find attractive as African Americans, Africans, Asians, Indians, Europeans, Latinos or whoever is often very particular to that continent, that region, that country, that city, that block. Beauty is such an individual thing—such a wonderful, particular, person-by-person thing—that has nothing to do with scientific formulas or anything that anyone can measure. How ridiculously worthless is it, then, to try to reduce an entire race and gender to some kind of value in a graph? To say that a billion women in one race suck because they don't look like the billion in another?

Ridiculous as I think it is, though, the kind of pronouncement made by the researcher in *Psychology Today* is just another in a long line of gut checks that, in this already youth/weight/plastic-surgery-obsessed culture, pound away at black women's self-image. It wasn't just the Rutgers women's basketball team that was hurt when Don Imus called the championship-winning team a bunch of nappy-headed hoes. And it seared like fire when John Mayer said he doesn't date black women because his peen is a racist—a quote that made many of his black fans, myself included, feel like he absolutely hates, with an unyielding passion, black girls. Hell, we even get it from our own: Dumbass Albert Haynesworth, a former pro football player who is African American, defended himself against sexual assault charges by saying he couldn't and wouldn't have groped the breast of an African American waitress because she's "a little black girl who's just upset I have a white girlfriend. I couldn't tell you the last time I dated a black girl. I don't even like black girls."

Deep, deep sigh.

Look, I don't need validation from Don Imus or John Mayer or dumbass Al Haynesworth or anyone else. But I am trying desperately to save my little girls. From the magazine editors who refuse to put brown-skinned girls on their covers and in their pages. From the TV show producers who shovel shows on Disney and Nickelodeon without a care in the world that viewers hardly ever see characters of color. From the music and movie industries, which, even when brown girls are involved, put greater stock in light skin and long, flowing weaves. From the book industry, which seems like it'll suck blood from a stone before it backs books featuring black children.

And I'm trying to save my girls from celebrities and singers and pro ballers and anyone else who has a microphone and especially researchers who will, by any means necessary, tell them that their brown skin and thick lips and pudgy noses and kinky hair make them ugly and manly and unattractive and undesirable.

But you know what? That's a whole lot of fighting. A whole lot of guarding. A whole lot of explaining. A whole lot of counterbalancing.

And on days like these, I get tired, y'all.

And wish that my beautiful black girls and I could just . . . be.

—*MAY 2011*

CHAPTER 16

The Sun Will Surely Make You Black

THIS IS WHAT I DID FOR FUN when I was a kid: I read. I cornrowed my doll's hair. I read some more. I annoyed the crap out of my brother. And I waited anxiously for Fridays, when my dad would let me ride shotgun while he drove around town, paying his bills. When we got back home, I read. Again.

Going outside to play wasn't an option. Not that I grew up somewhere nefarious where little black kids had to negotiate dope boys or gang warfare to play in the park; I was raised on Long Island, in a nice house, on a nice street, with a really nice backyard. And I refused to play in it. There were bugs out there. And nobody wanted to play with me, anyway. And I took it really seriously when my parents said that I should avoid playing in the sun because it would only make me blacker. Heaven knows I didn't want to be any blacker. At least that's what my parents used to tell me.

Come to think of it, that was the general line of wisdom from the 'rents whenever there was discussion of doing outside activities. You don't want to go to the pool, you'll get blacker. Why on earth would we go to the beach? You just get black there. Play kickball? Outside? In the sun? Don't you know you can get black doing that?

I got so used to them coming up with excuses for why they didn't want to accompany me to outside adventures that soon enough, staying inside became the modus operandi—a lifetime one, really. Several decades, three kids, a dog, and a mortgage later, I still don't do backyards or bikes or parks or beaches too much. I sit out on the deck overlooking our expansive back yard and immediately start swatting at invisible bugs. I'll toss the ball around with the girls and then find at least five reasons why I need to be back in the house. Alas, enjoying nature is not natural to me.

I never really thought about why that is until last week while Nick and I were watching the *Today* show and Nick was reminiscing about how he used to see the celebrity who was being featured, Kevin Bacon, out in Central Park a lot, playing with his superstar wife Kyra Sedgewick and their kid. And I remember thinking, "Really? A celebrity in Central Park? Just playing with his kid and stuff?"

I pondered this for quite some time (probably way too much time considering how much work I had on my plate, but I digress), and got to thinking about how many times I saw my parents just, like, playing. And it dawned on me that the last time I saw that was, um, well, never. I've never in my *mumbles age to herself* years on this earth felt my father's hands on the small of my back, pushing me higher and higher on the swing as the air swirled around me, kissing my face. I've never seen my parents curl their toes in wet, salty beach sand or splash in the rush of seawater slamming against the shore. I'm quite sure that I've never seen my father's hand in a baseball mitt, or his sneaker booting a soccer ball toward a makeshift goal, or his fingers lining up against the stitches on an oval-shaped piece of pigskin.

It wasn't natural for them.

Wild stab at it, but I'm going to guess that they didn't like being outside because they both grew up in the South, on farms, where being outside was all about work, hardly ever play. The two, longtime factory workers when I was growing up, also worked ridiculously long hours and, to be fair, spent their free time trying to rest up for more work on the job, or church. Not much else.

Thank God and my sporty husband that the great outdoors

is much beloved by my girls, even if their mother is a total lame. They think nothing of tumbling out of the garage, tennis rackets, soccer balls, basketballs, bikes, sidewalk chalk, jump ropes, and hula hoops spilling from their arms, for the great driveway/backyard/front yard adventure. They erect humongous chalk cities replete with cafes and movie theaters and gas stations and malls on the concrete, and perform Olympic-worthy somersaults and back flips on the trampoline, and duel to the end in front of the soccer goal, sometimes with their bare feet digging into the dirt and grass while our dog, Teddy, looks on lazily. Sometimes, they hang upside down on their humongous Rainbow swing set, talking about everything and nothing. They dig in the dirt and make seven-course mud dinners and pile rocks and study bugs, even as they scurry across their little fingers. Neither finds any of this gross.

I do. But I don't try to steal their joy. I just watch them from afar, wondering if I would have been a different, more outdoorsy girl if I had neighbors like them to drag me outside (a few of mine were forbidden by their mothers from playing with "the niggers," as discussed later in this book, promise), or parents who just, like, made the time, a few minutes or so to enjoy the backyard they'd worked so hard to have.

My Daddy lives in Virginia now, on the land he tended when he was a young boy helping his father with his burgeoning wood business. My father tends to his grass like a mother does her newborn; the greatest of care is extended to practically every blade. He's always been a stickler about his lawn, my Daddy. Except now, he encourages his grandbabies to run circles on it and cartwheel across it and dance in the rain of his sprinkler until they are drenched and giggled out and all shriveled up. Occasionally, my girls talk their Papa into taking them to the local park, where the walking trail stretches so far you can stroll from Virginia to North Carolina without leaving its bountiful borders. He walks with them slowly, steadily, tossing bread toward the ducks and geese and pointing out the beauty of the great outdoors.

He doesn't point his face to the sun—you can get blacker that way—but he doesn't stop my daughters from doing it.

I don't judge him.

I understand.

And I promise myself to try to do a little better.

—*DECEMBER 2008*

CHAPTER 17

The Part Where My Daughter Starts Hating Her Bootylicious Butt

S O THERE'S THIS STUDY out by *Glamour* magazine that says women, on average, have at least 13 negative thoughts about their bodies during the course of the day—one for every waking hour. That sounds about right. Why, I had at least four during the 15 minute stretch between the time I got out of bed and the time I towel dried after my shower:

> Me looking in the mirror: Your skin looks horrid; what's with all the dark spots?

> Me brushing my teeth: Dude, you *gotta* go get some teeth whitening, stat.

> Me on the scale: Ugh. For the next week, you need to eat air. Nothing else. Just air.

> Me after my shower: Well damn. Remember when your thighs were juicy but reasonably thin and your stomach was stretchmark-less? Blame Mari and Lila for the travesties. Oh, and pull out the fat jeans.

Of course, if some man—namely, my husband Nick—had said any of this to me, I would have shanked him spouse-style: no clean underwear, home-cooked meals, or nookie for, like, ever.

And he would have been gotten a nice, terse phone call from my divorce attorney. Still, knowing full well that no one should ever say such things to any woman, I let those thoughts about my own self invade my brain virtually every time I pass by a mirror, sans repercussion.

What's worse is that my baby, Mari, is doing this, too. At age 11.

Curious about what they truly think about their bodies, I asked my daughters if they ever think bad thoughts about themselves during the course of the day. Lila, a.k.a. Hollywood, gave me an emphatic no. Apparently, she's perfect just the way she is and believes it to the core. This is a good thing. I think. Until, of course, her head doesn't fit through the door.

But when I asked Mari the same question—if she has negative thoughts about herself—she looked up from her homework and said, quietly, earnestly, emphatically: Yes.

> Me: Really?
>
> Mari: Yes.
>
> Me: What do you say?
>
> Mari: Well, when I get dressed in the morning, I always think my butt is too big.
>
> Me: Long. Blank. Stare.

I mean, hearing that shook me to the core. And hurt like hell. Because I thought I'd been working overtime to make both my daughters believe that they are perfect just the way they are—a process that began before they were even born. When Mari was in my belly and a sonogram revealed that she was a girl, I vowed to make sure she could see her beautiful brown self reflected in on the walls of her love-filled room. Back then, baby décor featuring black children was scant (still is, really; when's the last time you saw, say, a picture frame, bedspread, or growth chart decorated with brown ballerinas?) and so I ended up making a border of picture frames filled with pictures of her family on the wall next to her crib. And when she was born, I filled her bookshelves with picture books written by and featuring people of color, and let her fall asleep to lullabies sung by the likes of Kathleen Battle, Stevie Wonder, and Donny Hathaway. So she could feel her people deep down in her little soul. So she could know for sure that her color, her flavor, her heritage, her history is astoundingly, unapologetically beautiful.

Despite the "black is beautiful" indoctrination, we faced our battles; it took for what seemed like forever to get her to learn how to love her hair. And I've worked overtime to get my babies to appreciate their bodies, because Lord knows I didn't want them to face the storm of harassment and ridicule that nearly broke me when I was an impressionable little girl.

Still, somehow, all the cheerleading I've done on behalf of my babies means nothing when my 11-year-old, curvy and bootylicious and thick like me, pulls on her jeans in the morning. She's decided in her young mind that having a booty and thick thighs is a problem—a problem exacerbated, I'm sure, by the fact that she's surrounded by other 11-year-old girls who are thinner and decidedly less bootylicious and who, in turn, can still fit into the cute-but-smaller-cut clothing in the children's departments and uber popular tween stores like Justice.

But how do I switch her mindset on this? How do I tell my 11-year-old that, ironically, the very thing she hates about herself is the very thing that will get her lots of positive but, in some cases, unwanted attention when she's a teenager and the boys start smelling themselves and get up the nads to speak to her in an, I'm-a-guy-and-I-think-you're-cute-and-we-should-kick-it kind of way? I mean, I don't let her watch BET or listen to sexually suggestive Hip Hop or R&B music and so, quite conceivably, she's not really aware yet of the black male obsession with big booties—that really, at the base of it, having junk in her trunk is a *good* thing. (BTW: according to the March 2011 issue of *Allure*, big butts currently are a national male obsession, no matter the race. Shout out to JLo, Kim Kardashian, and them.) And frankly, that's not really the message I'm trying to pass on to my 11-year-old, who is still, thankfully, happy to be a little girl and not some over-sexualized Hottentot Venus.

Still, I want her to appreciate her gift and not obsess over it like I did when I was a little girl and my mother tried her best to get me to hide it and my best friend's mom called me fat because of it and I felt awful about the size of a part of my body that, no matter what I did, would not get smaller.

I'm trying to find the words—the appropriate ones for my tween. Somehow, appreciate and feel good about your body, no matter that it feels so trite. Mari is smarter than that and way more thoughtful. I have to make the words count. And hell, I'm stuck.

—FEBRUARY 26, 2011

CHAPTER 18

How I Help My Daughter Embrace Her Beauty

HER PRONOUNCEMENT sent a chill through my spine—heavy and wintry and thick. "But I look . . . I look . . . I look like a boy!" my daughter insisted, doing a slow wall slide down onto the kitchen floor, dissolving into a heap of tears and tantrum, torn to pieces over, of all things, her hair. She wanted expensive extensions so that her locs could swing below her shoulders. I wanted her to love the hair growing out of her head, exactly as it is, because it is beautiful and unique and hers. My gentle "no" did not go over well.

Now, when I was 15 and worrying about what the popular girls looked like and who the boys found attractive and how I could overcome this dark skin and these thick thighs and this big ass and this kinky hair and all this straight-A, honors brain and the bargain store clothes, and actually get someone to, like, notice me, there were no tears. No fallouts. Bettye, my mother, didn't play that. School was for the learning. Work at the factory was exhausting. Ain't nobody had time for a daughter's whining over hair and boys.

Buck up. Ignore them. Focus on what is important. That's what my mother said. That's that old-school parenting right there. It worked for Bettye. The effect it had on her daughter? Untenable.

See, the thing about being 15 is that the hormones are raging and that independence is kicking in and comparing yourself to the knuckleheads around you is inevitable, and the more you look at your reflection in the mirror, the more things you find wrong with yourself. Especially if no one is pointing out all the things that are right. Left unattended, self-esteem can wither and wrinkle up like a sticky raisin in the sweltering summer sun.

I know this for sure. Spending half of a lifetime picking myself apart and thinking everything that falls between the top of my head and the soles of my feet was wholly inadequate gets you really clear on such things. I hated me. And I hid myself under baggy clothes and a bare face and sensible shoes, insisting that being pretty wasn't important at all—that being the smart, do-it-all workhorse was the only thing that mattered. I was 40 years old before I effing figured out that wearing makeup, dressing in cute outfits that fit and flatter, and taking pride in rocking an adorable hairstyle is not about impressing or competing with anyone else. It's about me loving me. I would just as soon chop off my hands and sever my own tongue than knowingly let either of my daughters feel the way that I did all those years before I had that epiphany. To spend even one second thinking they are not enough.

So I make the conscious decision to water.

Some days, this is not an easy proposition. My child is 15 but still, she is my baby. Just a few more years and she will be off on her own adventure—college, a career, her own home, maybe marriage and a few babies, too. My time with her—these very specific, hands-on, face-to-face, heart-to-heart moments—soon will be no more.

So in a rush of emotion and brain throb and yes, a smidge of fear, I am thinking—always thinking—about what else needs to be taught. This is how you iron a skirt with pleats. This is how you shop for groceries on a budget. This Roy Ayers song is the backbone of Mary J. Blige's "My Life," one of the best songs about black girl angst ever written. This is a good credit score, that guy is an example of a good dude, over there is a neighborhood in transition and that's not necessarily a good thing. My baby listens.

Sometimes she asks questions. Sometimes she's annoyed by the lessons. I know that she tucks it away and recalls it when it counts. But the beauty stuff, that is new.

Luckily, girlpie is open to growing responsibly—to blossoming into her own at a reasonable pace. She's stunning, really, with these gorgeous copper brown locs cascading all around her chocolate face, the perfect exclamation point to her Beyoncé thickness—all curves and hips and booty and black girl goodness. Some days, I look up and I see her there and my heart skips a beat. My daughter is blossoming into a beautiful young woman. She just doesn't know it yet. So I tell her so. This is important. Confidence—the ability to square the shoulders and hold your head up high and celebrate your own loveliness—is as exquisite and rich as a Ruby Woo lippie. Looking good helps you feel good about yourself. Feeling good about yourself makes you feel secure. Feeling secure makes you feel like you have superpowers—allows you to get to the deeper business of feeling beautiful on the inside. This is important, too.

I help my daughter do the work.

That work started from the womb, you know—from the moment that cold, sloppy goop was slathered on my belly and the sonogram revealed her to be a girl child. I hung pictures of our family on the wall all around her crib, so that every day she opened her eyes and looked up she would know she is loved. I filled her library with books featuring characters that look like her, so that she could see herself in the imagination of others. I rocked her to sleep to the sounds of Stevie Wonder and India.Arie and Earth, Wind & Fire and Lauryn Hill, so that she could feel love of self deep down in her soul. And every day—every single day—I told her how pretty her hair is, how I adore her face, how her skin is the same amazing color as "mahogany," my favorite Crayola crayon, how strong and beautiful are her legs and her shoulders and her arms and her booty and back and feet.

Still, she has her moments when she doesn't like what she sees. We all do, of course. That's human. But at 15, it's especially challenging, particularly when you're a black girl with natural hair, being raised by parents who don't allow the weaves, risqué clothes, and makeup masks that seem to be the fashion and beauty choices of practically every other black girl in our local public high school here in Atlanta. I will not be sending my kid to the 10th grade looking like an extra on the set of *Love & Hip Hop.*

This, of course, is what was behind the desperate quest for loc extensions. I get it. It's not easy to be different in a sea of cultural clones. But rather than let her fall victim to trying to be like everyone else, I wiped her tears and held her in my arms and we made a plan for how she could look more like how she wanted to look. We worked first on ways to style her locs, Googling pictures and watching YouTube how-to videos for cute looks she could pull off on her own. Then we dove into her wardrobe, discussed her personal style, and added key pieces that represent it. She is now allowed to wear eyeliner and lip gloss with a smidge of color. And when she walks out the door to school, this kid is totally badass—in a way that is age appropriate and a full reflection of her burgeoning personal style.

Of course, she is really clear that there is so much more to being a beautiful person than looking pretty and dressing fly. Being intelligent, outspoken, thoughtful, kind, hardworking, independent, and more is a given. Each is a work in progress. She's getting those in, too.

But being beautiful on the outside will, for sure, help her get to the deeper business of being beautiful inside. And loving herself for her, and nobody else. —*AUGUST, 2014*

CHAPTER 19

Raising 14-Year-Olds Ain't for Punks

S HE STARTED HIGH SCHOOL last week—left this house in a ball of nerves and excitement and fear and delight, curious about this new, independent path she was about to walk, sans her mother's hand to squeeze during the scary parts.

I offered to make her an omelet. She wasn't hungry. I plotted to drive her two blocks to the bus stop. Her father told her to walk, and *he* parked a block away, in case her ride didn't show up. She did let me take a picture of her dressed in her first-day-of-school outfit, a custom we've practiced every year since her first day of school at age two. For this small piece of ritual, I am grateful. I stared at her picture through tear-filled eyes for at least an hour.

It's so cliché, that whole "where did the time go—it feels like she was born just yesterday" thing. Still, the feeling is visceral. True. And really, it's starting to sink in that the sweet little ball of chocolate I carried in my belly and pushed through my loins and fell totally, helplessly, eternally in love with all those years ago is a baby no more.

My firstborn child, my Mari, is 14.

There's so much that comes with this age, things that make all the other milestones we parents tend to fret over—sitting up, first words, first steps, potty training, dry nights, first day of kindergarten, first lost tooth, and all of that—feel trivial. After all, when they are little, they are dependent and vulnerable and our jobs as parents, as my mother once told me, is to "keep the kids from killing their fool selves." We grown-ups are in total control. We know it. The children know it. There is no pushback. It is what it is.

But, my God, how those dynamics change when our babies mature and those hormones are in full effect and they start smelling themselves and get behind the wheel of their own thoughts and emotions and desires and . . . pull away. My Mari has her own ideas on how she wants to dress, what she wants to listen to and watch, how she feels about the world around her and how she wants that world to really *see* her. My once sweet and helpful and bubbly child has morphed into straight lines and sharp edges, with an attitude and opinions and a fierce hunger for independence—the kind that comes with a challenging of rules and a demand for self-sufficiency and a smidge, too, of secrecy.

I remember 14 and I (try to) understand—(try to) acknowledge that she has the right to like what she likes (within reason) and think how she thinks (with logic and evidence to back it up) and feel what she feels and that those likes and thoughts and feelings may not necessarily sync with mine and this is okay. As she evolves, so, too, do I.

So I loosen my grip. Just a little. Enough to let her wings flutter. For her to make her choices—in clothing, in friends, in the things that interest her. She can walk across the street from school to the Starbucks and the earth won't stop its rotational spin. She can talk to her best friend on FaceTime until midnight on a Friday and let out that primal teenage girl squeal when a Mindless Behavior video comes on TV and ignore her little sister and, for hours at a time, answer questions with one-word mumbles and the sun will still rise in the morning. She can choose the blue shirt instead of the green, wear the stretch jeans, purple shirt and sneakers instead of the hip pink dress and sensible flats, and rock her hair cascading on her shoulders instead of the gorgeous topknot I think shows off her beautiful face, and she will still be . . . mine.

Still, allowing this feels like she's taken one of my lungs. She's learning to live. I can barely breathe knowing that while I am still a part of the equation she uses to factor how to legislate her space in this world, I am no longer the absolute in my 14-year-old's math.

So this is where trust comes in. Not only in my daughter but in my own parenting skills. My husband and I have done our best to steer our daughter down the right path—our family path. We have reminded and still do remind her constantly that the world is bigger than our little corner of Georgia, that a hairstyle or a stupid, ratchet reality TV show doesn't define her or her blackness, that the price of her shoes or the label in her shirt is no measurement of her worth, that books and art and culture are as necessary as air and the only time she should ever stop learning and challenging herself is when she is gone from this earth. And as she navigates high school, this new terrain of peer pressure and hormones and boys and no-nonsense teachers, I want—really need—my Mari to know that she has a voice and opinions and feelings and an experience that is valuable and important and true. And that she has the right to use them. To have them heard. Respected.

Silence is not an option.

This is all to say that raising a 14-year-old ain't for punks. It's when parenting gets *real*. I face the challenge head-on, knowing that my one-on-one time with my daughter will be cut short in just four years, when she heads off to college. I accept the challenge, too, because I am hopelessly, helplessly in love with her.

This will be so until dolphins fly and parrots swim the sea. Always. —*AUGUST 2013*

The Nuts and Bolts of Parenting Black Children

CHAPTER 20

Baby Ear Piercing: Maybe It's Just a Cultural Thing—or a Mom's Prerogative

I HAVE NO EARTHLY IDEA how old I was when I first got my ears pierced. What I do remember, though, is that I got them done in a hole-in-the-wall shop in a Long Island strip mall, and I was sitting on a long metal table, and my mother was holding me down while some strange lady with a huge Afro and a bigger needle lit the sharp end of the needle's tip with a lighter and then rubbed my ear with ice. You know what came next. I want to scream right now, just thinking about it.

So traumatized by the experience was I that when one of my holes closed months later, I refused to get it pierced again. I ended up rocking one gold hoop in my right ear for what seemed like forever—looking like a little chocolate Mr. Clean with bangs and bows—until a friend of mine made me feel like a sucker for having only one hole and dragged me to the mall, where, this time around, I got popped in my ear with a piercing gun. Right. That mess hurt, too.

Still, practically the moment I found out the child in my belly was a girl, I turned to my baby books and BabyCenter.com for intel on when it would be safe to get my daughter's ears pierced. The books said I could have them done after her first two rounds of vaccines; the pediatrician confirmed but said I should wait until she was at least four months old. On her four-month birthday, her godmother and I took her to a high-end jewelry store and, while

I held her close and stroked her back, a technician pumped two gold balls into Mari's lovely ears.

Three years later, when my Lila was six months old, our pediatrician numbed her little ears with some solution and pierced hers, too.

Despite my own trauma, I thought nothing of piercing my daughters' ears because, well, that's what we do: We have babies and if they're girls, we braid their hair, dress them up really cute and get their ears pierced as soon as it's safe to do so. There was none of this, "Oh, it's her body and she should decide if she wants it altered" talk—no "Let's hold off until some arbitrary birthday so we can get our mother/daughter bond on" discussions. It was what it was. The alternative—baby girls with naked ears—never was an option.

Frankly, it wasn't for any of my friends with daughters. Specifically, black daughters. I honestly cannot recall one single African American, Latino, Indian, Middle Eastern or other girl child of color that my daughters have been friends with who doesn't have pierced ears.

But I certainly can recall the big deal that was made when a few of my white friends were taking their elementary school-aged daughters for their big ear-piercing days, which, now that I think about it, usually fell on special birthdays, like double digits or whatever. And there are quite a few of them that do not have their pierced ears, too. Apparently, our affinity for piercing our daughters' ears isn't necessarily widely held by white moms. Which might explain all this brouhaha sweeping across the mom blogosphere of late, with bloggers squaring off on whether ear piercing constitutes torture.

No, really—I'm dead ass.

It started with a letter in a *Pittsburgh Post-Gazette* advice column, in which a concerned reader likened piercing babies' ears to "borderline child abuse." That same day, a blogger at CaféMom's

The Stir cosigned, calling parents who pierce their babies' ears "cruel." And, well, yeah—shots fired. Our girl Roxana Soto of *Spanglish Baby* broke down the significance of ear piercing in the Latino culture and basically told folk they should just mind their own business. And *Today Moms*, the online parenting portal for the *Today* show, tied up the various arguments into a nice, neat little post, weighing all the opinions and doing polls about it and whatnot.

And over here at *MyBrownBaby*, I'm still trying to figure out what the hell the big deal is. It's an ear piercing, for goodness' sake. Not a tattoo. Not a female circumcision. Not anything that is harmful or, if you get the piercing done early enough and by a professional, even painful or memorable. I'm pretty positive that Mari and Lila cried more over vaccination shots than they did over their ear piercings (which were much more evolved than the iced-ear/needle method I suffered through as a preschooler). I checked in with Mari and Lila at dinner last night and both of them actually thanked me for hooking them up when they were infants, because they don't remember any of it, which is way cool by them. So unaffected by it is Mari that she asked for a second piercing, and I happily obliged her, so long as she promised that she would clean and care for her new piercing on her own. She agreed. The second piercing is gorgeous—every bit as pretty as their first piercings from when they were babies.

Here's a thought: how about, if you don't think it's cool to pierce a baby's ears, when you have a baby girl, don't get her ears pierced. If you want to save it for her 10th birthday, then do that. But really, passing judgment on us moms who pierce our babies' ears? Yeah, not fresh. —*JANUARY 2013*

CHAPTER 21

Young, Gifted, and Black

D EAR MARI AND LILA,
    Some day, you'll understand. . . .
Why my heart swelled with pride when you, Lila, trotted onto the bus, looking all smart and independent and cool-girl charming on your first day of fourth grade. . . .

And why, two weeks later, I burst into sloppy Mommy tears when you, Mari, slammed the car door and trudged to the junior high school building, the warm, salty water nearly blinding me as I willed myself to drive away and leave you, my newly minted middle schooler, to the business of being a seventh grader. . . .

And why, years later, I still fret over your first-day-of-school outfits and your new backpacks—insist your hair looks just so and all manner of eye boogers are gone when you slide into your seats at your new desks, in your new classrooms, with your new teachers. . . .

And why your daddy and I insist on clearing our overwhelmed calendars to press our palms into those of each of your teachers at the veritable avalanche of "welcome to your kid's school" parent/ instruction nights spread out all across town.

These are the things most mothers do, granted, but my motives are inspired by my past—one filled with memories of parents who had neither the education nor the time nor the wherewithal to really be there for their studious daughter. Please understand, Gamma Bettye and Papa Jimy valued education like no other; they came from a generation of African Americans born and reared in the South—where black babies were relegated, by law, to substandard schools and books and jobs and neighborhoods and services. And so the first chance they could, they hightailed themselves up North, first for jobs, second to find each other, and third to give their children the opportunities they were denied when they were little. But for your grandparents, there was no time for PTA meetings and school bake sales, no know-how when it came to writing essays or figuring out tough algebra problems, no advocacy with teachers. Maybe they felt like they couldn't handle it. Perhaps it was what parents like them did in their time—trust that teachers are professionals capable of doing their jobs without parents getting in the middle of it all.

This tactic worked for the most part. But there were many times when I needed them to just, like, read the landscape—help me chart where I should be and what I should be doing to get there. On a few occasions, I needed them to fight for me—to understand that just because we were living in the suburbs and in a decent school system didn't mean their daughter was immune to stereotypes, racism, sexism, or adults who had low expectations for kids who looked like me.

What my parents did well, though, was inspire. They told me consistently that I was capable of doing anything I put my mind to—that I could be anything I wanted to be.

Most days, that was enough to get me through.

But I don't want you to have to settle for "enough." I need you to walk into your classrooms, shoulders squared, chins up. Ready. To be the brilliant girls your father and I are raising you to be. So there is absolutely no confusion between the two of you and all of the statistics that suggest children who look like you come from homes where parents don't care about education, aren't involved in the classrooms, and are incapable of raising kids who can finish school strong.

You are not statistics.

You are young, gifted & black—beautifully so.

And I vow this day and every day after that to remind you and anyone else listening to understand these things—by showing my commitment to your education through classroom volunteering, by making sure you both participate in extracurricular activities that make you well-rounded students, by helping you navigate the social scene of little girls and (gasp!) little boys, by surrounding you with like-minded families who are doing the same for their babies, by reminding you on a consistent basis that you are brilliantly and abundantly blessed with beautiful minds.

In other words, you can count on your daddy and me to be there for you at every turn, no matter what. We won't embarrass you—at least not on purpose. And I'll try to keep the tears to a minimum. But there are no guarantees.

Some day . . . you'll understand. —MARCH 2015

CHAPTER 22

The Most Important Advocate

T HE WORDS STUNG—the action as devastating as a Mike Tyson roundhouse. The guidance counselor, charged with gathering up official transcripts and recommendations for the scholarship application I was submitting, insisted that because she didn't think my grades and SAT scores were good enough to win, she couldn't be bothered with photocopies and praises. That I was a straight-A student who ranked 20th out of a senior class of more than 600 was of no consequence to her. The local community college. That, she made clear, was where I belonged.

I had bigger ambitions, though. Bigger than community college. Bigger than the small Long Island town where I grew up. Bigger, obviously, than what that guidance counselor envisioned for me.

Still, I couldn't count on my parents to explain this to her. In the minds of my working class mom and dad, who had little money and less education, the sole stretch between Suffolk Community College and Yale was the mileage between their physical locations. And if the teachers and counselors, whom my parents trusted like they did their doctors, said I should take whatever class and participate in whatever extracurricular activity and go to whatever college, well, who were they to argue? Those people up at the school taught physics and algebra and got kids to college, for goodness' sake. Surely, they knew what they were talking about.

A few weeks later, that same counselor refused to release

documents I needed for a second scholarship for which I wanted to apply, an action that moved me to put in a teary collect phone call to my mom. I begged her to step in. She did. And, after a closed-door meeting with the principal, she left not only with my transcripts, but the cash she needed to send in my application via overnight mail.

I won that scholarship.

And we learned a valuable lesson—both my mother and me. For her, the lesson was in the power of speaking up on her child's behalf. For me, it was learning that it's never a good idea to leave the educational destiny of my children solely to the teachers—that as a parent, it is my duty to watch, listen, ask questions, work the system, and speak up for my kids.

Now that I'm a mother and I've spent a few years sitting in the little chairs at parent/teacher conferences and room mom'd my way through five of Mari's six years in school and all four of Lila's, I recognize that not all parents think this way. That for every day I've spent in the classroom, getting to know the teachers and the principal and, most importantly, letting everyone within earshot know that my girls are brilliant and willing and able to learn and I expect nothing but the best for them, there are 10 parents who barely pay attention to their children's homework, never come to parent/teacher conferences, and put in the absolute minimum when it comes to volunteering in their children's classrooms.

I'm not going to lie—I've stood in judgment of those parents. Like, what does it take to check a third grader's homework? Or donate some chips to the class party? Or talk to the teacher about what the standardized test scores mean for your kid—before critical decisions are made about your child's future? I get it: parents are working/inundated/intimidated. But shouldn't participating in the education of your child be at the top of the list of parental priorities? Eat, exercise, sleep, and learn. That's what kids do. That's what we parents are supposed to help them do.

This was certainly on my mind as details of a huge standardized test score scandal swept through the Atlanta Public School system. A state report revealed that, for years, almost 200 teachers in dozens of schools throughout the huge district had been giving answers to students and changing answers for them, too, on the Criterion-Referenced Competency Tests (CRCT). Teachers and principals implicated in the scandal say they did it to protect their jobs; passing CRCT scores meant students got promoted to the next grade, which meant the kids were learning, which meant the teachers were doing a good job teaching them and being rewarded for their efforts. But while the teachers who cheated were winning, it was the students, ultimately, who lost. And that is the shame of it all.

Of all the coverage I read on the scandal, the quote that stood out to me was from one teacher explaining why she participated: "I had to give [students] the answers; those kids were dumb as hell."

As a mother, that hurt me to my core. Because this woman was in charge of those babies. And thought nothing more of them than that they were unteachable idiots who didn't deserve to be taught.

I'd like to think that my mom Spidey sense would have sniffed this woman out—that I would have instinctively known this woman meant to do my kid harm and that something wasn't right if my child was coming home with failing grades but passing the CRCT with flying colors.

This is what parents do. You pay attention and you stand up for your kid.

I talked about this with my friend Gretchen, a former middle school teacher who, as an instructor at a local university, readies college students for elementary classrooms, and she made a salient point: for all-too-many poor urban and rural parents, teachers, like doctors, are gods. You don't question them. You do as they tell you. And when the bill—or, in the case of your child/student, a report card—comes, you put it in the pile and deal with it when you can, if and when you have the means to deal with it.

And I get that. I do. Because I came from a home with parents who didn't understand algebra and physics and biology, who knew nothing about personal essays and college applications, who didn't know the difference between Suffolk Community College and Yale. Who simply trusted the teachers and the counselors to have their child's best interests in mind.

Well, not all of them do.

And while there should be shame for those teachers, I really wish that the parents of the students had been paying closer attention to what those teachers were doing to their babies. You don't need to know algebra to do this simple math: you can't fail third-grade reading and arithmetic, but pass standardized reading and math tests with flying colors. I guess wishful thinking would have you believe that maybe some brilliance snuck into your kid's head the night before the standardized tests, even though she'd consistently done poorly on classroom tests throughout the year. But reality should tell you this simply is not likely.

My gut tells me that someone should have caught this long before the state of Georgia did. I wish it were the parents. —*JULY 2011*

CHAPTER 23

Indulging My Daughters' Passions

W HEN I WAS LITTLE, I wanted to play the piano like Stevie Wonder and speak French and travel to faraway places like California and Hawaii and Harlem. Alas, these things happened only in my mind. My parents, after all, were factory workers—bound to blue collar paychecks, limited vacation days, and a work schedule that stretched from sun up to can't see. Lack of time, money, and sleep meant I could be a world-traveling, French-speaking, piano-playing wonder child only in my dreams.

Of course, I hold no ill will toward my parents for this. But I promised myself that things would be different for my girls—that they'd grow up having known the excitement of exploring a new land, learning about new cultures, and, above all else, having their wishes indulged.

It's not that I spoil them, mind you. There's a big difference between caving to every little whim and coaxing and encouraging their love of something new. Like, when Lila got it in her mind that she should take ballet lessons because her best bud Maggie was dancing and got to wear fancy tutus, well, no, there were no ballet lessons. Ditto when Mari begged for a cell phone because all of her friends had them.

However, when Mari became borderline obsessed with the marching band that performed during the halftimes in her big brother's football game, and I noticed how she seemed to really dig the warm notes in Miles Davis's *Sketches of Spain*, her father and I rushed out and rented a trumpet and signed her up for lessons. And when she and her little sister started showing a genuine interest in helping me whip up fancy meals and started searching Google for science projects they could hook up in the back yard on their own, I obliged them with summer classes at a kids' cooking camp and a hands-on, get-dirty science program. Both encouraged my daughters to trust their instincts, be independent, and really fall in love with learning.

And my girls are still talking about their summer vacation to Paris, a trip we saved up two years for after Mari, Lila, and their big brother, Mazi, made clear that they had the Eiffel Tower in their sights.

My daughters are older now—16 and 13—but this philosophy of mine hasn't changed one bit. In fact, it's only solidified now that my girls are old enough to truly know what interests them beyond a passing fancy—skills, subjects, and explorations that might very well turn into lifelong passions.

For instance, Mari, my 16-year-old, has more than a passing fancy for practicing medicine. She's been talking about being involved in the sciences since she was six, and years later, told her seventh-grade science teacher that she wanted to be a doctor. Her proclamations remained so intense that her father and I switched her out of a private school into our local public high school that has a curriculum that prepares students for specific disciplines, including biomedical careers.

In keeping with her desire to be a physician, Mari applied for and got a coveted spot in a summer medical internship program for high school students that she learned about from one of her teachers. She's spending her summer working as an intern at a local hospital that has a hands-on training program for young doctor hopefuls. Two weeks into her internship, my daughter already has learned how to do ultrasounds, watched doctors conduct CT scans, helped intubate a patient, and witnessed the intake interviews of trauma and psychiatric patients. Needless to say, this intensive immersion program is giving her an up close look at what it takes to do the job and really consider early on whether being a doctor truly is what she wants to do for a living.

My younger daughter, Lila, who has her sights on being an agent, will be getting her own immersion program of sorts when she spends a week working with my literary agent in her office in upstate New York. She'll be checking out manuscripts and book proposals, watching the decision-making processes that go into choosing which prospective authors will get agency representation, helping to prepare book auction letters for publishing houses and, the part that excites her the most, doing the math on the cut the agency will get for the book advances they score for clients. What can I say? The girl's been obsessed since seeing the movie *Jerry Maguire* last year and has been taking weekly phone lessons on "agenting" from my agent. So what more perfect way to let her experience the inner workings of promotions than to arrange for her to see all of it in action firsthand?

When they're not getting hands-on experience in their respective fields, my girls will be working their way through a list of summer reading to keep their minds nimble. Mari is also taking an online advanced algebra class to qualify for a few AP courses in her junior year. Lila will be completing math work her dad solicited from the seventh-grade math teacher, just so that she can keep what she learned fresh as she prepares for a more intense math workload in the eighth grade. No summer slide for them if we can help it—unless it's at a waterpark.

Of course, none of this stuff—the trumpet lessons, the cooking classes, the science camps, the trips to faraway places—was cheap, believe me. And Mari's internship was highly competitive (there were only 15 spots and hundreds of applicants), and not everyone has a literary agent, much less one willing to indulge a child's passion to wheel and deal on behalf of artists.

But any parent can tap into their own resources and ingenuity to get their children the valuable up close look at the careers they think they're passionate about. If your child likes art, take them to the local museum and, in addition to checking out the master works, see if you can schedule some time with one of the museum's curators. That person would be a fount of information on the many different careers a kid interested in art could pursue. Consider tapping your own friends for their valuable insight; call on your doctor friend to take your kid to work for a day or out to lunch to talk about careers in medicine. Or stop by your local fire station to arrange for a friendly firefighter to talk about his job. And doesn't everyone have that savvy uncle or distant cousin who has a slew of contacts? Call him up. My Lila, the brave one, simply picked up the phone and asked my agent if she could hang out with her to learn the business. Truly, it was as simple as asking. Sometimes people will say "no," but many more times they'll say "yes" because they like sparking the interests of kids. Really, it's as simple as that.

I know that each experience opens my kids' eyes to possibilities, and makes clear to them that the world is so much bigger than our tiny sliver of Georgia, and that there is tremendous value in being indulgent if it means you'll find refuge in knowledge, pursue your passions, and experience the beauty of trying something new. —*JULY 2015*

CHAPTER 24

Easing Mommy Guilt: 20 Quick Ways to Connect with Your Baby When Time Is Short

E VEN TO THIS DAY, more than a decade later, I remember what it felt like—that gnawing, desperately unsettled, perpetually unsatisfied, I'm-totally-failing-my-baby feeling I had when I was juggling a full-time job, a burgeoning book career, a young marriage, and new motherhood, all at the same time. I was a features editor at *Honey* magazine—a demanding job that called for long hours, some late nights, and ridiculous commutes from a Manhattan office to our home in New Jersey. Mornings always were rushed as I'd make the teary-eyed day care drop-off and the mad dash to work, and I'd get home barely in time enough to kiss my baby goodnight, let alone feed her dinner, bathe her, read to her, and love on her the way I wanted to. The nanny, a grandmotherly woman whom we hired after a couple of disastrous run-ins with bad babysitters, was a terrific nurturer for my Mari, then about two. But she was caring for, nurturing, and loving on my baby—what I should have been doing. What I longed to do. Quitting my job wasn't an option—or a desire. I liked working and I was excited about where my book career was headed. But I wanted more from my relationship with my baby. Much more. I'm sure this is what I was thinking when Nick drew up The Mari List. The Mari List was a manifesto of sorts—an inventory of activities he whipped up to help us bond with our girlpie in meaningful ways, even if our time together was limited. I don't quite remember if we did anything on the list, but when Nick found a copy of it in his computer files—more than a decade after it was drawn up(!)—my heart melted remembering why we made it up and especially where my mind was in the whole work-life balance struggle at that specific time in my motherhood journey. For sure, I was thirsty for a true connection with my daughter. Anyway, I thought it would be fun to share with you The Mari List. Perhaps you'll find here something fun and adventurous to do with your babies. Or, like me, you'll reminisce about the fun you had with your children when they were wee-bits. Enjoy!

THE MARI LIST

- When coming into the house, we can gather up a bunch of leaves and try to recreate their various colors using the crayons we have at our disposal.
- We can get Play-doh and see who can make the best sculpture of a dog.
- We can see who can jump on one foot the most times without falling.
- We can roll a ball back and forth to her on the floor.
- We can see who can balance a book on the top of our head the longest.
- We can get a gigantic piece of paper and have her lie down and trace Mari, then cut it out and have her draw Mari's entire body inside.
- We can look through magazines and cut out every picture we see of a dog, then decide which one is the biggest doggy and which one is the smallest, which one is the prettiest, which one looks the meanest.
- We can get dolls and start showing her how to braid their hair.
- We can get together our instruments and everybody play a song while we record it.

- We can go outside at night and count the stars in the sky.
- We can count all the trees we see on the way to Amberlena, or all the blue cars.
- We can have Mari create her own songs to sing, using the people and places she loves.
- We can look through magazines for pictures of people and determine whether they are happy or sad.
- We can get a stack of five books and see how many times we come across a bird, or a kitty cat, or a Mommy, or a Daddy.
- We can plant a seed that becomes Mari's plant, and have her water it herself every day.
- We can learn a new song every week with Mari, with everybody in the family having to learn it so we can all sing it together.
- We can teach Mari how to pat her head and rub her tummy at the same time.
- We can teach Mari tongue twisters, like "Peter Piper picked a peck of pickled peppers."
- We can play catch with a ball, or even a pillow.
- We can build a tunnel with the pillows and have Mari crawl through it.

—APRIL 2013

CHAPTER 25

School Dress Codes Unfairly Target Black Girls & I'm Tired of It

T HE THING IS we live in midtown Atlanta, ground zero for the culture that birthed *Love & Hip Hop*, the Nae Nae and every rapper's favorite stripper haunt, Onyx, so it only makes sense that the little girls around our way roll to the local high school with Ruby Woo-painted lips, bird-wing-length eyelashes, weaves and wigs swinging, and clothes that are questionable at best. Thanks to some serious home training and a boatload of common sense, my 15-year-old knows better than to even think about leaving the house dressed inappropriately. But that didn't stop my freak-out the other morning when she tried to leave for school in a crop top that, when she raised her arms, showed off a little belly.

"Oh, no ma'am," I said, shaking my head violently from side to side. "I'mma need you to either grab a jacket or put on a tank top if you're going to wear that shirt, babe. Get to it."

Be clear: I'm no prude and I'm not raising one. And on any other occasion—going to the mall, heading to a friend's house, attending a party—what Mari was wearing would have been perfectly fine and age appropriate. But she was heading to school. Specifically, a public school. Where girls in general and black girls, in particular, seem to be targeted for strict wardrobe policing by everyone from the principal to the janitor. The last thing I want to do during the course of my day is run up to the school with a change of clothes for my daughter, or, worse, have her dressed in somebody's old, nasty clothes from the lost-and-found bin and sent to in-school detention for running afoul of the school's dress policy.

To be fair, I think the dress code is reasonable: skirts and shorts need to be the same length as a student's longest finger when hands are placed at her sides, spaghetti straps are not allowed and sagging and hats are a no-go for the boys. I wouldn't want to see anybody's drawers, boobs, or booty while I'm working or studying either.

Where it gets dicey, though, is in the part of the rules that morph and stretch and twist to fit the awfully subjective whims of people who view black bodies through a wholly different lens. In their eyes, an African American girl with 36Cs, thick thighs, and a bubble booty rocking the same regular ol' crop top and a cute skirt as her white counterpart becomes a nubile slut intent on turning out her teachers and fellow students in the nearest stairwell or beneath the bleachers. She is sexy. Inappropriate. Wild. Loose. And must be tamed, by any means necessary.

I saw this with my own eyes when my niece, a curvy little Beyoncé Barbie, got sent home practically once a week over her clothes, many of which I purchased and thought were just fine, but that would draw the attention of one particular vice principal and a couple of teachers who would fall just shy of calling her a slut-puppy for wearing what every other teenager was wearing. On a couple of mornings, Nick and I actually went over to the school and watched the students walking into the front doors and took note that many of the white girls were wearing outfits infinitely more scandalous than my niece, but no one seemed to see fit to send them to the disciplinary office. They were too busy clocking what the black and Latina girls were wearing. For sure, whenever we got called down to bring our niece a new outfit, she'd be sitting in that office seething next to a room full of girls of color, all of whom were deemed "inappropriate" by whoever took it upon themselves to decide this.

It was disgusting.

And to have my daughter tell it, it's not too much better at her school, either. "There's a lot of white girls who wear some scandalous clothes and they never seem to get in trouble for it," she said. "Like, ever."

Granted, there are a few stories floating around about white girls facing the wrath of school administrators jumping all over them for their clothing choices. A school superintendent in Noble, Oklahoma, came under fire for suggesting that some of her female students were "skanks" for dressing too provocatively for her taste and later forcing other female students to bend over to gauge whether their skirts and dresses were too short. (For the record: had someone forced my kid to bend over so she could take a look at her crotch area, y'all would be crowdsourcing my bail right now.) And a bunch of courageous middle schoolers in South Orange, New Jersey, took their school administration head-on with their #IAmNotADistraction campaign, arguing that rules focused solely on restricting girls' outfits to keep boys from being "distracted" made them feel like they're "bad" and need to cover up and that boys are "animalistic" and can't control themselves.

They have a point. But add to the mix school suspensions and other punishments that black girls face disproportionately to their white counterparts, and those deeply rooted stereotypes of black girls and women as hypersexualized, vulgar, ghetto, animalistic, titillating hookers become a convenient and deadly weapon that slashes and burns our daughters' educational opportunities, disciplinary records, self-esteem—even prom nights. It becomes more than a cute hashtag and a rally for the right to wear a bikini to a school-sponsored pool party. It becomes a matter of more odds stacked against our daughters' education and graduation rates and certainly their right to . . . be.

I don't want that for my kid. She doesn't want that for herself, either. And so even on the hottest days, she wears pants instead of shorts, sweaters over crop tops and tanks, and avoids leggings like the plague. And frankly, that makes me hot as hell. —*AUGUST 2014*

CHAPTER 26

On Free Range Parenting and Letting Kids Run Amok

MY MOTHER WORKED during the day and my father worked the overnight shift and there was some overlap between their jobs, particularly if overtime was involved, so there were plenty of days when my brother and I were on our own and we had to make good use of basic skills to get ourselves home from school, let ourselves into our house, fix ourselves something to eat, and find ways to entertain ourselves until a grown-up finished working and came back home. Today, this would be called free range parenting.

In my house, it's called unnecessary.

My husband and I moved to Georgia from New York 10 years ago and became full-time authors and freelance writers so that we could raise our children the way we saw fit: with love and attention to detail—the kinds of details we couldn't swing while working jobs that sucked up all our time and left us little time to do the things that mattered to us. Have dinner together. Put our babies to sleep at night. Relax on weekends instead of trying to squeeze in every chore we couldn't get to during the week between the guilt-trippy playtime we plotted and planned to make up for leaving our kids to the nanny to raise. Spend quality time just . . . being.

That desire to be a hands-on parents hasn't changed now that our daughters are older. We are there for them—on the sidelines at the soccer, softball, and basketball games. In the audience at the band concerts. At the dinner table, talking about our day and everything else, from politics to boys to race to tricky friendships. Taking the time to parent our kids.

Some call this helicopter parenting. I call it . . . parenting.

Apparently, our way makes others feel some kind of way, as evidenced by the audience response to an interview I participated in on NPR's *Weekend Edition*. In "What Kind of Parent Are You: The Debate Over Free Range Parenting," freelance journalist and mom Katie Arnold and I were charged with discussing the case of Danielle and Alexander Meitiv, a Silver Spring, Maryland, couple that let their 6- and 10-year-old children walk a mile to a local park and play, unsupervised, for an hour—a move that got their children snatched by Child Protective Services. Katie stated that she thought it was okay for the kids to go to the park to play alone, so long as their parents taught them how to get there and trusted the kids could make it back home at an agreed upon time. I made clear that I thought it was a "bit much" to trust that kids that young would be safe.

I went on to reveal that when it comes to my own daughters, I have some pretty strict rules for navigating the park here in Atlanta: They can go, but only with either me or their dad present, and once inside, they can go off and ride their bikes without me, but they can only do so for a limited amount of time before checking in.

Well, according to the commenters on the NPR site, I am an overbearing shrew raising two henpecked, overly dependent scaredy cats who will be so socially stunted that they (1) won't be able to navigate college campuses or life on their own, (2) will be terrified of strangers for the rest of their lives, (3) will be dependent on me to accompany them to job interviews, dates, and all other manner of life because their overbearing mother didn't allow them their independence, and (4) a bunch of other stupid shit that does not bear repeating here.

Apparently, these judgy folks all grew up in households with parents who let them hop on their bikes at age 10 with nothing more than PB&J sandwiches and pocket knives and tramp all through the neighborhoods and in the parks and woods, exploring and getting into stuff and discovering their idyllic world, and every last one of them, too, allows their tweens the same freedoms today in 2015, sans concern for strangers or safety out here in these streets.

Let them tell it and free range parenting is magical, and giving a half damn about your child's safety makes you a crap mom.

You know what? I'll be that. I live in the urban center of a city, near the 189-acre Piedmont Park, off a main thoroughfare with easy, quick access to three different highways, in a place that is known to have one of the highest rates of children trafficked for sex. The average age for girls sucked up into the sex trade here in Atlanta? Between ages 11 and 14.

My daughters are 12 and 15.

Yeah, yeah, yeah—our nation's crime rate is the lowest it's ever been and child kidnapping statistics are lower than our perception and kids are more likely to be hurt in their own homes than they are by strangers in the street and blah, blah, blah. Yes, this all makes sense. Until some guy is looking at your shapely 15-year-old and trying to holler because he likes her phatty. Or some teenager likes your 12-year-old's bike enough to knock her off of it and take it for himself. Or someone is hungry enough to stop a kid on a quiet, secluded bike path and take her ice cream money—or, God forbid, something else. Or until you're making a plea on the six o'clock news for someone to call the police with any information they might have on your daughter's whereabouts.

Don't get me started on the racial factor here—about what comes when black boys are running or riding their bikes through communities where "neighbors" automatically look at them with suspicion and assume they're criminals (RIP Trayvon), or they're subject to the stop-and-frisk policies of police departments, or a mother, out of necessity rather than for play-play, leaves her young child at home while she works, only to have "well-meaning" citizens dial up CPS and accuse that mother of neglect. The stakes are high when black children and their parents are involved and the system gets them into their line of sight.

I'm not a betting person. I don't take chances when it comes to the two people who are more precious to me than anything on this earth. They are smart, beautiful girls who are still learning how to be, with parents who love them hard and strong and want the best for them and think very deeply about how we can grow them up to be incredible, accomplished, independent women. Game changers. We simply do not subscribe to the idea that the sole way to teach a child independence is to let them roam the streets unsupervised. Yes, I feel this way about six-year-olds. And 10-year-olds. And 12- and 15-year-olds too.

You have your way.

We have ours.

And I won't feel ashamed for it, either. —APRIL 2015

CHAPTER 27

Hanging Up the Belt: Finding My Way to the Time-Outs

S HE WOULD LOOK AT YOU with those eyes.
Piercing.

Glaring.

Cut. Throat.

That's how my mom shut down all kinds of kid shenanigans. The Look all but screamed, "If you don't stop it right now, I'm going to (insert indictable child abuse offense here)." The mere threat of bodily harm made me straighten up and fly right; Bettye had to beat my behind one time only for me to know she wasn't to be played with. Shoot, even kids who weren't her kids knew that when Deaconess Millner gave you The Look, you best get back on the good foot, lest she take you down into the church basement for a little talking to that maybe involved little talking and a lot more hand movement than you'd care to experience.

The Look was no joke.

I tried looking at my kids that way. They laughed at me.

Tried spanking them both, too. Mari looked at me with a fear in her eyes I never want to see again; truly, I'd rather be respected than feared by my eldest daughter. When Lila got her butt smacked, she damn near giggled in my face. Or maybe she cried. Then went right back to what she was doing, like my hand never connected with the fatty part of her leg. Which is the equivalent, in my book, of giggling in my face.

Basically, the childrearing techniques that worked for Bettye don't necessarily work for me and for good reason. My mom, along with my father, raised two children in the era of Reaganomics, stable factory gigs, good health benefits, and New Edition. Child Services would doggone near high-five the 'rents for tapping that butt. Today, we moms are trying to survive the policies of The Decider. Competing with Lil Wayne lyrics. And working hard to raise up smart, well-behaved, conscious children, sans the beat downs despite the odds. And without the Department of Youth and Family Services breathing down our necks.

Somehow, my mother figured out how to discipline us without the benefit of ScreamFree Parenting coaching, without a parade of child-rearing segments on the *Today* show, without a subscription to *Parenting* magazine. I think my brother and I turned out pretty okay. But there's something to be said for some of these newfangled techniques we loudly, resoundingly rail against in the company of our parent peers and especially our own parents, but secretly practice behind closed doors. I readily raise my hand and admit that I give Mari and Lila the straight ice grill when they cut up in front of old black folks—you know, to make it seem like I'm capable of laying the smackdown. But at home, when the over-50 crowd isn't watching, time-outs and talking tos are practiced regularly. Even crazier, sometimes they actually work. Take, for instance, yesterday morning: I was packing Lila's backpack and discovered not only was she trying to smuggle her Nintendo DS to school, she's swiped an entire pack of Now and Later from my private candy stash. Had it all up in the front pocket, like it was hers.

Now please understand, playing with my Now and Later candy is like playing with my emotions.

But I didn't trip. When I was six, that would have been grounds for a sound butt whooping, but all my six-year-old got from me was a firm, "You know you're not supposed to take your games to school, and you didn't ask to have any of my candy, which means you stole it from me. So now you don't get to take snack to school, and you don't get to play your DS for three days. Now eat your cereal."

Well you would have thought I'd skinned her with a foot-long switch; the tears were flowing like the Nile down into her Cinnamon Toast Crunch. But when girlfriend realized I was unmoved by the drama and unbowed from my punishment pronouncement, she shut up the noise, ate her cereal, accepted her fate, and, as we walked hand-in-hand to the bus stop, she apologized for ganking my stuff.

And just like that, the drama was over. No cowhide needed to be swung. No shoes needed to be flicked. Nobody had to go out and fetch a branch off the tree. I didn't have to mean mug or even raise my voice in anger (my one crutch I'm really trying to work on is the yelling, y'all, honest!). She got a simple punishment. And it was over.

If only it could be this easy every time.

We'll see.

In the meantime, I'll be practicing The Look in the bathroom mirror. You know, to break out in case of emergencies.

—*JANUARY 2009*

CHAPTER 28

Hello. My Name Is Denene Millner and I'm a Screamer.

I DON'T MEAN TO HOLLER and yell like a banshee when my kids get out of line. It just, like, happens.

Usually, I yell after I've asked them nicely five times to do something—like move their crap off the kitchen table or straighten up their rooms or go to sleep already because it's 10:30 p.m. and I put you in your bed two hours ago and I'm tired, dammit, and I want to give your father some so that I can pass out from exhaustion.

Or I might yell if they start sparring each other like they're prepping for the next Tyson vs. Holyfield heavyweight fight.

I'll definitely raise my voice at my kids if they're defiant. Talking back gets my goat. Pretending you didn't hear me when I know good and doggone well you did takes me over the edge.

And so I pump up the volume.

I yell.

I figure my kids are lucky. My mom didn't mince words. She'd look at you with those piercing, glaring eyes, first. And then she'd commence to inflicting bodily harm. A belt. A fresh switch off a tree. A shoe. Bettye wasn't to be played with.

I tried spanking my kids. Hitting them wasn't the answer. Plus, it just didn't feel right. I'm smarter than they are. I can figure out how to discipline them, surely, without inflicting physical, grown woman pain on their kid bodies.

Punishing seems to work, now that they're older. What do

you know about making a 17-year-old write a typed, 10-page essay on the plight of African American males when he cuts class? Or demanding a 10-year-old write a two-page apology letter to her little sister, whom she's just mistreated? A half-hour banishment to the bedroom sans TV works wonders for getting Lila's attention, for sure. Smack her butt, yank her hair, pull out her toenails but please, please, *please* don't take away chatterbox's ability to socialize or she'll just, like, die.

Of course, talking it out is a reasonable, grown-up response to kids who misstep. My husband, Nick, is very good at this. I am not. My brain is overtaxed, what with the working and the scheduling and the chauffeuring and the homework and the after-school activities and the cooking and the cleaning. Coming up with clever ways to calmly explain to the 10-year-old why she shouldn't "bottle feed" her doll red punch on the freshly cleaned beige carpet, or tell the 13-year-old it's not a good idea to put Silly Putty in her armpits isn't exactly the first thing that pops into my mind when it comes to disciplining my kids.

And I do see the benefits of lowering the volume, as duly noted in the *New York Times* piece, "Screaming is the New Spanking," and I'm working on being better about this disciplining thing.

But my name is Denene Millner, and I'm a screamer.

And some days, this is just the way it's going to go down in my house.

Okay? *OKAY?!*

Okay. —*AUGUST 2012*

CHAPTER 29

Hitting Kids Is Dead Wrong

L ET ME ASK YOU THIS: Has the whole world gone mad? No, seriously, were the tickets to Nuttyville discounted at the local Walmart or something? I ask this because my Facebook newsfeed has been filled with stories of grown-ups beating on their children and actually celebrating it as *the* go-to parenting tool to raise good, well-behaved, well-mannered children.

One Texas family court judge, William Adams, who oversees cases of child abuse, was shown in a YouTube video using a big leather strap to beat the pee out of his 16-year-old daughter—a whooping that lasted for close to eight minutes. Her infraction: she downloaded video games and music. As views of the video climbed to more than six million and the nation, buoyed by the daughter's appearance on the *Today* show last week, debated the merits of spankings and just how far is too far, Adams's family finally released a statement questioning his daughter's motives for releasing the video and apologizing to his community for "the interruption and inconvenience" she caused by releasing the video—suggesting that her father may be a teeny weeny bit of a damn lunatic. Who probably shouldn't be deciding child abuse cases. Or let anywhere near her 10-year-old little sister.

Adams's video popped up just a few weeks after another man released his own video of a "disciplining" session he had with an eight-year-old boy who was being punished for cutting up in class. In that video, 25-year-old Devery Broox captions and numbers his discipline techniques, which include using a strap to beat down his little charge, shaving off the boy's "swag"—i.e., his eyebrows and key chunks of his hair—and then sending him outside for a brutal boot-camp-style workout that would make the Navy SEAL team run home crying to their mamas. He kicks off the video with a screwy missive about how many black men are in prison and how it takes a village to raise a child; please note that I learned about the video via a morning radio show, on which the hosts and every caller cosigned his techniques under the guise that if we don't beat our kids, the "system" will. Um, okay. I'm not going to rehash statistics of increased drug use, criminal violence, and prison rates for adults who were abused as children; you can read them on Childhelp.org.

The icing on the child abuse cake came in the form of a story in the *New York Times*, which focused on a pastor, Michael Pearl, his wife, Debi, and their "parenting book" (I use the term "parenting" *very* loosely), *To Train Up a Child*. The tome, which has sold 670,000 copies and is said to be a favorite of Christian disciplinarians who cling to the "spare the rod" scripture, gives directions on how to beat six-month-olds with switches and, according to the *Times*, describes, "how to make use of implements for hitting on the arms, legs or back, including a quarter-inch flexible plumbing line that, Mr. Pearl notes, 'can be rolled up and carried in your pocket.'" The *Times* wrote the story about the Pearls because their book showed up recently in the homes of three separate parents who face charges of beating their children to death.

Long. Blank. Stare.

When, my God, *when* are we going to stop this madness? When are we going to recognize that the "fine line" everyone speaks of between discipline and abuse really isn't a line at all, and that hitting a kid for any reason is just plain bad parenting? Don't come at me with the, "I was spanked and I'm fine" thing. I was, too. And you know what it did for me? It made me scared to death of my mother. It made my brother defiant and rebellious and sneaky. It made one of my cousins a lifelong criminal. Another cousin, so angered by the years of abuse he endured as a child, refused to attend his own daddy's funeral. I'm sure their outcomes from that "discipline" have been and are being repeated all across this country—playing themselves out in the courtrooms and the prison cells and the crack houses and psychologist offices of our homeland.

Seriously, folks: want to know how to discipline your kids? Get your parenting skills up. Read a book. Google it. Phone a friend. Buy a clue. Use your adult brain to figure out how to get your kid to do what you want and what you say without hitting them. You're smarter than children. You do NOT have to resort to physical violence to check a six-month-old or a six-year-old or a sixteen-year-old. Like, ever—point blank period.

And if it sounds like I'm being judgmental, it's because when it comes to hitting kids, I am. We *have* to do better by our babies.

For tips on healthy ways to discipline your kids without physically abusing them, check out SpareTheKids.com, an organization started by Stacey Patton, a child abuse survivor. I also encourage you to read *MyBrownBaby* contributor Michelle Bond's piece, "A Reformed Spanker Reveals Why She Wishes She Would Have Spared the Rod." Each will make you think doubly hard about disciplining kids and finding ways to do so without hitting.

—NOVEMBER 2011

Loosening Pop Culture's Hold on Black Children

CHAPTER 30

Damn That Lil Wayne

S O I'M IN THE CAR on my way to Target with my daughters when I realize I pulled out without my pack of homemade kid-friendly/mom-approved CD mixes. Now, this isn't an issue if I'm driving alone; I simply tune into talk radio (Warren Ballentine has my ear during morning errands, Michel Martin's NPR show *Tell Me More* is on in the afternoon, and I smile all the way to my exercise torture er, African dance class listening to Farai Chideya's *News & Notes* in the evenings). But Mari and Lila neither understand nor appreciate the finer points of intelligent black thought on the RNC convention and the Kwame Kilpatrick fiasco (hey, they're nine and six—have an exhaustive talk about Sponge-Bob, Raven-Symoné, or snot, and they're all in). So I turned on the radio. It was nine in the morning. I live only about five minutes from Target. How bad could it be? I asked myself as I punched in my local R&B station.

And wouldn't you know, on comes Lil Wayne's "Mrs. Officer," with Bobby Valentino contributing a chorus of police siren noises and dirty talk about what he's going to do to the lady cop when he gets her in the backseat of her ride. It took Lila, the six-year-old, all of three seconds to tap into her inner Beyoncé and join along, singing about getting "all up in ya" and making "that booty sing," topped off with Bobby Valentino's *wee ooh wee ooh wee*. She sang with much gusto and way too much glee.

When I tell you I almost crashed the ride into a ditch trying to change the station?

A rambling blackout lecture immediately followed—I think the words "inappropriate" and "mommy's not mad, really," and "since you're not grown," tumbled from my lips. But mostly, I remember the look of confusion and fear on my baby's face. *Why*, I could tell she was wondering, *is my mother bugging out over a song?*

Here's why: because Lil Wayne with his "Lollipop" and Bobby Valentino with his *wee ooh wee ooh wee*, and black radio, with its devil-may-care playlists blasting in the afternoons for all of the Elmo set to hear, are k-i-l-l-i-n-g this generation's ability to hear and appreciate good music. And frankly, I'm tired of it.

Now don't get it twisted: I love Hip Hop and R&B. I'm a product of it in every way—sat by the stereo in my parents' basement every Friday night listening to Red Alert and Mr. Magic; blasted Run DMC, LL Cool J, and Rakim from my stereo in my college dorm room; got through my year living away from home and on my own listening to A Tribe Called Quest, De La Soul, Pete Rock & CL Smooth, Mary J. Blige, and Jodeci; covered some of the greatest lyricists and singers ever as an entertainment reporter for the *Daily News* in New York. I'm prone to blasting Jay-Z, Nas, Lupe Fiasco, T.I., Ludacris and music by countless other artists whose lyrics are astounding.

But the babies don't know nothing about them.

That's grown folk music.

And I just wish that somebody who has control over what's played on my local radio station when I'm driving the kids to school, or picking them up from swim practice, or driving them to Target would act like they know this, too. I mean, I distinctly remember as a teenager listening to legendary radio jock Frankie Crocker explain why nobody would ever hear Marvin Gaye's "Sexual Healing" before 9 p.m. on his watch. The subject matter, he said, wasn't for the kids to hear. I didn't fully comprehend what the big deal was, but then, Crocker wasn't talking to me, right? He was helping out my mom and dad, who, while at work, just didn't and couldn't control what my brother and I were listening to on the family stereo.

Sadly, there are no Frankie Crockers, it seems, on the scene today, just deejays who are quite happy to tell moms like us that they just play what the audience wants to hear and if we don't like it, oh well.

With apologies to black radio, and at the expense of sounding like a played-out mom too old to recognize cool when I hear it, I'm just going to go on ahead and tune out when my girls are in the car, thank you. And for other moms considering the same, get yourself a good kid-friendly, mother-approved R&B and Hip Hop hits playlist both you and your kids can enjoy the next time you're in the car, without fear. —*SEPTEMBER 2008*

CHAPTER 31

Don't You Wish Your Daughter Was Hot like Tyra?

I KNOW THERE'S A SPECIAL PLACE in Mom Hell for me, but I let my daughters watch *America's Next Top Model*. (There. I said it out loud.) Every Wednesday, without fail, they dutifully take their baths, get into their jammies, and line up on the carpet for their must-see TV—an hour's worth of need-a-macaroni-and-cheese-I.V. stat!-thin model wannabes, climbing into fabulously impractical clothes, slathering their faces with more colors than a 64-pack of Crayolas, and striking poses that defy all realms of logic. My girls are all in from the recap/preview in the first minutes to the very last moment when Tyra sends the weakest mannequin packing. They roll their eyes during the makeover meltdowns, crack up over the model mishaps, shake their heads and tsk-tsk when the contestants get catty, and pour over the elimination photos, making predictions about who had the best shot, and, naturally, who sucked (my word not theirs).

Of course, the model who takes their breath away every week is the queen of it all, Tyra Banks. Tyra alternately clowns her subjects and plays mama, shows them the tricks of the trade, and disses her model-wannabes hard when they fail to live up to her supermodel standards. And my girls cling to Tyra's every word and talk about her slick dresses and her perfectly-coiffed hair and how pretty she looks when she smiles with her eyes.

They. Love. Them. Some. Tyra.

Total stans, I tell you.

So much so that one recent week, Mari asked me if I thought she looked like Tyra.

Now, please understand: I'm the president, CEO, and executive director of the Mari Is the Most Beautiful Girl in the World (Next to Her Little Sister) Fan Club. She's a delicious little girl—got these thick, juicy lips, and high cheekbones, and these incredible chocolate-brown eyes, framed with sleight eyelids that make her look like she's got a little Japanese in her family. Nick and I recognize that when this kid hits her teens and gets the Beyoncé booty and hips going, it's a wrap. Rifles. Threats. Intimidation. We plan on using the full arsenal to keep the boys at bay.

But my baby doesn't look like Tyra.

Nothing of the sort.

(I guess I should be happy that she didn't say she wanted to look like Paulina Porizkova, or Heidi Klum—that she picked a black woman as her ideal beauty. I mean, at her age, I wanted to look like Farrah Fawcett. That's another essay.)

But since I'm a stickler for keeping it real, I had to tell her: "Um, no, baby. You don't look like Tyra."

No matter that I broke the news real gentle, no matter that she had no verbal response, the defeated look on Mari's face spoke a thousand words. It was the look I remember seeing in the mirror when, as a little girl, I'd examine my eyes and lips and skin and hair and wonder why I just couldn't measure up to the prettiest girls in my school—the ones who seemed to get all the attention, all the boys. In my daughter's face, I saw vulnerability. In telling her she didn't measure up to the woman she idolizes, I had, in effect, delivered a southpaw uppercut to her self-esteem.

So I went into damage control mode told her the truth, but added a little sugar to make it go down better. Tyra is beautiful, but so are you, in your own special way. I told her how much I loved her twists, and adored her cheekbones, and the way her face was shaped like a perfect, juicy apple. "You are lovely, sweetheart—a beautiful, special little girl." I told her. "But if you want to be like Tyra, be like her in the ways that mean something. Be smart. And independent. And fierce. And run your own business and call your own shots and be the one to tell everyone else what to do. Tyra is dope like that. And I know you've got the beauty to be as pretty as her, but I also know you have the smarts to be just as successful as she is, too. That's what makes you special, and that's how you can be like Tyra."

She was quiet.

Thought about what I said for a moment.

And then she smiled at me with her pretty eyes.

Crisis averted (for now).

And I'm still in the running to be the Next Top Mom.

—NOVEMBER 2008

CHAPTER 32

We're Too Bougie for BET

S O I'M CELEBRATING the New Year (read: recovering from my sister-in-law's smokin' hot/spirit-filled/sweat-your-hair-out New Year's Eve party) by lazing around and flipping through channels when I come across BET's *Notarized: Top 100 Videos of 2008*. I hesitate to watch it, seeing as my Mari, who is sick, is lying up under me. I'm a firm believer that nine-year-olds shouldn't be watching anything on BET, especially 12 hours worth of videos featuring half-naked girls, misogynistic lyrics, and just plain bad music. But like a mythical vampire hypnotizing me before he sucks the life out of my naked flesh, the half-naked girls, misogynistic lyrics, and just plain bad music mesmerize me, and I am quickly sucked into the horror show that is the modern-day rap video. The nine-year-old, who's made clear that her restorative powers can be found only in the crook of her mommy's right armpit, refuses to leave the room; rather than turn to yet another episode of *SpongeBob*, I decide to use *Notarized* as a teaching opportunity for the kid. I start the lesson with a few caveats, including that watching BET is:

A. about as healthy for her as a month of carb-filled soul food Sunday dinners.
B. about as appropriate as 100 adult-themed movie trailers.
C. the most stereotypically revelatory piece of black theater she'll ever watch again before age 17.

And then we watch.

"Why," I ask her during Akon's "I'm So Paid," "is every girl sitting around in a bathing suit while the men walk around acting important? Do you think they care about how smart she is? Or that maybe she has something to contribute other than her looks?"

"No," she says simply. "They need more clothes."

Smart girl. We watch some more.

"Why do you suppose," I ask her during Ace Hood's "Ride," "that the girl in this video is acting like she hit the lottery just because her boyfriend bought her some clothes? Do you think maybe she'll get in trouble for accepting his gifts knowing that he bought them with money he got from doing bad things to other people?"

"Yeah," she says, nodding. "She should get her own job so she won't get into trouble."

True. Such a smart girl. We watch another video.

"Why in the world," I opine, "would someone make a song called, 'Please Excuse My Hands,' and more importantly, why in the world would someone play it?"

"Uh, I don't know," she says. "It's kind of a dumb song."

"You think?" I ask.

"Yeah."

See? Real talk. This is why I love me some Mari.

Baby girl was stumped, though, by my reaction to BET host Alesha Reneé, who, between videos, was planning a catered New Year's Eve soirée. No, she wasn't scantily clad. No, she wasn't laying up under some man or shaking what her mama gave her in front of the cameras for the world to see, or warbling through an incomprehensive rap. What she was doing was just as bad, if not worse, than that. "What," she sniffed at a chef charged with serving up treats for her party, "is that?"

"It's a canape, he said.

"Hmm," she said, wrinkling her nose and eyeing the

bite-sized cracker creation like it was a spoonful of rat poison. "A canape, huh?"

Now, never mind that she and the chef wrongly pronounced the French word for a bite-sized appetizer *cah-NAP*, or that it took her two—*two!*—commercial breaks before she dared put the doggone thing in her mouth. It's what she said after she tasted the chef's creation that made me want to reach into the television and touch her: "Oh," she said after finally trying one. "I feel bougie."

The hell? What, if it's not fried or boiled to within an inch of its life, it's white people food? Did she just signal to all the black people watching that the fancy food the chef whipped up wasn't for us—that any African American who dares sample foods beyond the scope of what's considered black food is trying to be something other than black?

Come on, now. It's exactly that kind of thinking that would have all too many of us rejecting any food that's not a burger or Popeyes and turning up our noses at all of the wonderful cuisines found around the world. I guess she's that chick that would travel to Brazil or Egypt, Nigeria or Kenya or South Africa or Ghana, or Haiti or St. Lucia or Jamaica, and sustain herself on Big Macs and Kentucky Fried despite that every morsel of food to be found in those countries can be considered black food. Would eating tripe cooked in red wine (considered a South African delicacy) be bougie? Maybe griot (fried pork, a Haitian favorite) would be too much of a stretch for black folks to try? Ditto acarajé, the Afro-Brazilian delicacy of kidney bean paste fried in oil from the dendê palm?

I'm sorry, but even my six-year-old knows that you have to try a food at least twice with a smile before you reject it, because it's just perfectly ridiculous to confine ourselves to such a limited number of food options when the world is full of wonderful, flavorful, thoughtful, delicious food.

This, indeed, is just one way in which Nick and I try to get our daughters and son to look at our place in this global universe.

The world is so much bigger than our little corner of Georgia, and there is so very much for them to learn about other cultures, the way people live, the way they think. We enroll them in art classes so they can learn about the great artists of our time—the Picassos AND the Beardens. We let them take Mandarin lessons not because white people have their kids enrolled in those classes, but because we want our children to learn the beauty of a language and a culture they have little contact with. And we let them eat foods like sushi and falafel and curry goat and peanut soup and yes, canapés, because we don't want them to grow up and embarrass themselves on international television talking about, "Ew, what's a cah-NAP?" and then pronounce themselves bougie just because they tried something different.

You know what? I think that if Alesha Reneé were invited to the homes of Jay-Z, 50 Cent, LL Cool J, Mos Def or any other prototypically black performing artist who also happens to be a multimillionaire, everybody up in their mansions would know what a canapé is, and if Ms. Alesha were to sneak into their kitchens to see what their private chefs are preparing, she'd probably find some bougie food on the stoves, too. Indeed, a friend of mine traveled to the south of France and stumbled into a party where she saw 50 Cent wearing a $3,000 suit, looking quite comfortable eating the food and drinking the drink of the rich and global white folks surrounding him. There were no Timbs there. No baggy jeans.

And not a piece of fried chicken in sight.

And no one would fix their mouths to call 50 bougie.

This is what I tell the nine-year-old when she sees me grimacing and sucking my teeth at Alesha Reneé's ridiculous antics.

"She sure is making a big stink about trying that canapé, isn't she?" I cluck.

"Yeah," Mari says. "I don't know what's wrong with her; that cah-NAP looks good."

See? That's why I love me some Mari. —*JANUARY 2009*

CHAPTER 33

Fear of a Black Booty

B EYONCÉ'S 2014 GRAMMY AWARD performance of "Drunk in Love" with Jay-Z was so many things: sexy, racy, fierce, dope. Had me bodyrolling and warbling "Surfin' all on this good good" with my outdoor voice. And texting my fitness trainer for an emergency session and new game plan for how I'm going to look as bootylicious as B did dancing all up on her husband. The absolute last thing on my mind when she finished and hugged it out with Jay on the stage was that this woman—a wife, a mother, a businesswoman, an international icon—would be called a "whore" for doing her job and doing it well. But there it was, right there in the headline of a UK newspaper: "'Whore' Beyoncé angers parents with raunchy act."

Whore?

Word?

Apparently, the sight of Beyoncé's derriere exploded the Internet, with a gang of handwringing hags flapping their gums about how their kids' childhoods were absolutely ruined—*ruined*—by the 56th Grammy Awards opener featuring the hottest chick in the game. According to *Metro*:

> Horrified viewer Mandy Flores wrote on Facebook: "Aren't u a mother now!!? Thought u had class, how trashy and I couldn't even let my 8-year-old watch. U have never done anything like that! So disappointed."

Others quickly reached for the remote control, with JJ Boogie tweeting: "Opening Grammy
song performance inappropriate for young children. Thank you Beyoncé. #ChannelChange."

Another horrified woman said the 32-year-old
mum looked like a "wh*re on stage" at the Sta-
ples Center in LA.

Trashy? Horrified? *Whore?*

Now mind you, these are the same people who would turn a
blind eye to racist "art" depicting a white woman using a naked
black woman as a chair and applaud Miley Cyrus using black wom-
en's asses as props in a bizarre, crotch-grabbing, chicken-twerk
dance at the VMAs, but have a conniption when Beyoncé strad-
dles her phatty across a chair and sings about making love to her
husband. They're the same people, too, who would giggle about
how adorbs Justin Bieber looks in his DUI mug shot but would
nod their heads furiously in agreement when fellow tweeters call
pro NFL player Richard Sherman a thug and ape and nigger for
expressing his emotion after a game-changing play that sent his
team to the Super Bowl. And you best be clear that these same
people probably wouldn't have said a peep when a major media
outlet referred to then-nine-year-old Quvenzhané Wallis as a cunt
on the biggest night of her life, but probably had to be buried, res-
urrected, and given a bushel of throat lozenges to get over seeing
Janet Jackson's boob tassel in the 2004 Super Bowl halftime show.
Did any of those women call Pink a whore for showing off her
Brazilian bikini wax during her splits and sexy curtain twirling at
Sunday's Grammy performance? No?

See the pattern?

I'll tell you this much: I'm done—*done*—with all this righ-
teous indignation over the baring of black bodies and the demand
that black artists color within the lines of respectability drawn

specifically for us. (I'm tired, too, of black folks who quickly cosign this foolishness by dragging Beyoncé for looking sexy while daring to sing about explosive sex, complicated relationships, the beauty of motherhood, and finding her voice as a woman in a sexist world, or dogging out shows like *Being Mary Jane* and *Scandal* for showing the less-than-perfect, complicated lives of single black women.)

How about Beyoncé sang a song in a sexy outfit with her husband by her side? How about nobody was tied to a chair with their eyelids glued open so that they had to watch Beyoncé's Grammy performance in its entirety? How about if you have a TV, it probably came with some kind of control on it that allows you to turn to another channel or turn off the TV altogether so you don't have to see—gasp—a big black booty in a thong.

More importantly, how about eight-year-olds should have their asses in the bed at 8 p.m. anyway? Fact is, Beyoncé wouldn't have been able to "horrify" your children if you were on your job. I counter *Metro*'s FB trolling/reporting with some of my own—the wise words of my friend and fellow author, Joan Morgan, who had this to say about parents complaining about Beyoncé's dancing/singing/clothing/being:

> And so here in lies the other problem . . . There were PLENTY of things my parents wouldn't let me watch, listen to, participate in when I was eight. Moms Mabley played frequently in our house and so did Minnie Riperton. I was just told to go somewhere cuz it was grown folks' business. And not for nothing, when Sule was eight, he had a damn bedtime. But I guess that's how it goes these days. Beyoncé's now a whore because you refuse to parent.

Say that, Joan.

How about instead of calling another woman/fellow mom a whore, you read a bedtime book to your kid and tuck him in? Or try what we do in our house with questionable content: we use the DVR as our own personal censor by taping potentially racy shows and starting them 15 to 20 minutes late so that we can fast-forward through inappropriate stuff or pause programs so that we can discuss with our daughters what they're seeing and how they should be thinking about it critically. You'd be amazed at how receptive kids are when you're talking to them rather than talking at them. Or worse, covering their eyes while you pile on and call people foul names. Now that's confident parenting. *insert side-eye here.* —*JANUARY 2014*

CHAPTER 34

Confession: I Let My Kids Watch Reality TV

S O Y E A H, a day after talking all that yang about the *Dark Knight Rises* shooting and how I refuse to take my kids to adult movies, I have this confession to make: I let my daughters, ages 13 and 10, watch *Love & Hip Hop Atlanta, Keeping Up With the Kardashians, The Real Housewives* and a bunch of other messy, dead-wrong reality shows that litter our nation's TV channels.

I know, I know—this totally makes me a crap mom in your eyes, doesn't it? Like, what respectable mother raising girl children to be smart, respectable, decent, upstanding black women with a healthy dose of self-esteem, self-worth and self-respect, would ply her babies with the *Pimps Up, Ho's Down* scandal that is thick-tongued, stripper-turned-side piece Joseline Hernandez? Or the slash-and-burn, bullying ratchetness of *Basketball Wives'* Evelyn Lozada and Tami Roman? Or the "We Don't Do Much of Anything but Sleep with Black Guys and Collect Checks for Looking Pretty at Events" antics of the Kardashian clan? I raise my hand and admit it, right here, right now: every Sunday and Monday, Mari, Lila, and I kick Nick out of the room, sit down with our popsicles and popcorn and totally fall into the abyss of the curse-filled, glass-tossing, misogynistic, hood rat antics that light up Twitter feeds from Atlanta to Compton, inspire "get it off our TVs, please!" blog posts and online petitions and generally leave a nation of black women feeling like both VH1 and Bravo just hate our asses.

Please know: there is a method to my madness. I mean, I'm not going to lie—we are *thoroughly* entertained. But we're not watching these modern day soap operas simply for the fun of it. During the shows, I work the pause button on the DVR like nobody's business, stopping the action, sometimes mid-sentence, so that I can explain the ridiculousness, warn about the behavior and show my little ladies how to do it the *right* way.

When *Basketball Wives'* Evelyn tosses a bottle and jumps across a table to twist someone's neck, I'm telling my girls that under no circumstances is it ever okay to end an argument with fisticuffs. When Evelyn's castmate, Keisha, responds to Tami Roman's merciless bullying and theft of her purse by calling the authorities, I'm telling the girlpies, "Yes. Someone slaps you in your face? Takes your Louis Vuitton bag? Don't give them time to give you directions on how to respond or stipulations on how to get your property back. Call the cops. Period." When *Love & Hip Hop's* Mimi Faust stands out in the parking lot, demanding manwhore Stevie J. not to get in the car with Jumpoff Joseline, I'm telling the babies, "Don't ever stand around letting a man humiliate you like that. If he's bold enough to wave the next girl in your face, he no longer gives a damn about you. Have enough respect for yourself to chuck up the deuces and get on with holding your head high, knowing you gave it your all but *it's over.*" Basically, there's a whole lot of teaching going on in those hour-long bursts of tomfoolery—wicked shots of wisdom taken straight to the head.

Turns out, I might be on to something. A study published in the journal *Sex Roles* revealed that while two-thirds of a group of girls aged six to nine told researchers they want to look "sexy," their wholly inappropriate desires were not rooted solely in the mess they see on TV. Instead, the study said, it's "the interaction between media hours and maternal self-objectification that creates vulnerability for early sexualization." In other words, kids who were exposed to the Kardashians and had mamas who act like Kardashian knockoffs in the house were more likely to want to want to look like a sexy Kardashian. Other research, though, took it a step further by suggesting that girls who are taught by their mothers to look critically at media and given an alternative narrative to what they're watching are more likely to survive the gauntlet of sexualized images and stereotypes fed to them at every turn and, in the process, learn to think a lot more critically about the music, television, movies, magazines, and books they're consuming.

I'm convinced my girls are getting the lesson. Way better than I did when, after school and during summer vacation, I fell into the abyss that was *All My Children* and *General Hospital*—totally unchecked. Mommy worked during the day and Daddy slept during the day so he could work the overnight shift, so the TV was mine-all-mine and by age 11 or 12, cartoons totally took a backseat to the shenanigans of Laura and Luke and Erica Kane. You want to know confused? Consider how I processed the infamous "rape" scene between Luke and Laura—replete with sexy music and soft lighting and, a few episodes later, an intact relationship between the attacker and the attacked. Right.

Of course, I waited quite a while before I exposed my girls to this madness. Up until this summer, they weren't even allowed to listen to black radio, watch BET, go on YouTube, or download music and videos to their iPods without my express approval. All of it was simply too grown for the girlpies and I figured they were much safer watching Nickelodeon and Disney and taking in my premade, mom-approved music mixes. But I've raised my daughters well; their critical ears are well tuned. Not pitch perfect; they are, after all, still children. But with my guidance, they're getting there.

Criticism notwithstanding, I'll keep letting my girls watch the shenanigans on *Love & Hip Hop Atlanta*, *Keeping Up With the Kardashians* and *The Real Housewives*—remote in hand, pause button on my trigger finger, conversation at the ready. The lessons are there, laid out in Technicolor—lessons on friendship, relationships, motherhood, conflict and conflict resolution, business acumen, mother-daughter bonding, beauty, self-esteem, self-worth. And I don't want my girls to miss one single episode. Because really, they're worth it. —*JULY 2012*

HAIR STORIES
The Joys, Pains, and Politics of Black Children's Kinky Curls

CHAPTER 35

Kinky, Curly, Lovely Black Girl Hair

T HE TORTURE USUALLY CAME on Saturday evenings, in the kitchen. I'd be sitting on a stack of thick yellow phone books and a pillow, squished between my mother's knees; she'd be perched on the hard wooden kitchen chair, bent over and leaning in at some ungodly angle, trying hard to tame the kinky curls at the nape of my neck with gobs of thick grease and a scorching hot comb.

I can still hear the sizzle of the comb on my hair and smell the thick, greasy, burnt hair scent clinging in my nose. I can't tell you which hurt worse: the fire-red hot straightening comb or the pop my mom would give me with the wide-tooth plastic comb for not being still or screaming out in pain or breathing while she tried to "straighten my naps."

From there, it just got worse. Like when my Aunt Sarah would braid my hair into cornrows so tight I couldn't see straight. And when my mom paid a professional hairstylist to have my hair "relaxed" with skin-burning lye. And then there was that unfortunate time when my dad, left in charge of my hair while my mom spent a few weeks in the hospital, gave me a jheri curl. He read the directions off the box and went to work right there in the middle of the linoleum floor, just me and him.

Right.

This is the story of all-too-many brown girls everywhere—a story that some of us African American moms are desperately trying to change with our generation of daughters.

Which is why there was such an uproar when *Newsweek*'s Allison Samuels openly criticized Angelina Jolie, a white mom, for letting her adopted, Ethiopian-born daughter, Zahara Jolie-Pitt, sport hair Samuels said was "wild and unstyled, uncombed, and dry. Basically: a 'hot mess.'"

Now, I wasn't about to jump in the middle of the raucous debate sweeping like wildfire through the Internet; there's been enough piling on from both sides of the issue without me adding to it. (Should Zahara's hair be wild and carefree? Should Angie take a black hair care class or two so she can "tame" Zahara's hair? Why are we criticizing a four-year-old's hairstyle, anyway?)

But I will say that even as an African American mom, it's not easy being in charge of two heads of kinky, curly hair—not including my own—with little information, great trepidation, and horrible memories of the Saturday night torture. There were no books out there to help me figure it out when my girls were babies; all of the information in the parenting books focused on hair and skin that didn't look or feel like my girls'. I mean, I knew everything there was to know about how to care for a baby with thin, blonde hair, and it seemed like every product in the kids' shampoo section was made specifically for them. But what was I supposed to put in my baby's hair? What would keep it from drying out? How was I supposed to comb it? What was I supposed to do as the texture changed, sometimes just on one side of her head? Was it safe to braid it? Pull it into puffs? Put barrettes in it? And what was a nice but curt way of telling my mom's friends that my kid's hair was in an Afro, sans braids/puffs/hairclips/lye because I liked it that way and it was actually better for her?

Honestly, there still aren't any black children's hair care books out that explain it all, and while there are a plethora of black hair care blogs online (I'm a HUGE fan of Afrobella.com), mostly they focus on grown folk hair, not the delicate but thick tendrils of black children. Simply put: even if Angelina wanted to find new ways to care for and style her African baby girl's hair, surely, she'd be at a loss, 'cause I sure am.

And so we are left to our own devices. Black child hair care ain't easy.

Mostly, my girls wear their hair in twists, though occasionally, I'll have it pressed so that I can have their ends clipped. When it comes to maintenance, their hair care tolerance is light years different. Lila screams holy hell when I announce that her hair will need washing sometime in the next month; she's truly the most tender-headed child on the planet. The girl can go three weeks with the same twists—lint and dried grass and all manner of rug remnants intertwined in her luscious locks—and not give a rat's booty if it looks like complete madness. Just please, don't say you're going to comb it.

Mari is much easier. I still remember the first time Nick and I washed her hair; she wasn't even a week old, swaddled in a blanket, nestled in Nick's big hands. He held her head under the stream of warm water in the kitchen sink, and I rubbed baby shampoo over her curly hair. The girl fell asleep like she was in a spa. I can pull it, twist it, scratch it, and the kid is cool. But she's got a dry scalp condition that keeps me workin' day and night trying to figure out how to keep her head moisturized, shiny, healthy, and natural. Some weeks, I have to wash, condition, and style her hair twice, almost two hours' worth of work at each sitting.

I've spent exorbitant amounts of cash on hair products that promised miracles. When those didn't work, I put together my own rosemary oil, Vitamin E, glycerin, and water elixirs for Mari's hair, and shea butter and coconut oil concoctions for Lila's—mixtures wholly conjured up from a patchwork of advice and Internet research on how to care for African American hair.

And when I'm not researching and combing, I'm talking to my babies—constantly talking—about how wonderful it is to have natural hair, with its gloriously kinky, curly, poufy texture, soft like cotton, strong enough to break the teeth of a comb. How it doesn't need to swing to be beautiful. That Afros—whether loose and wild and free, or teased into a puff or twirled into two-stranded twists like those rocked by Malia Obama—are the fire.

Nobody tells little black girls such things.

No, we grow up with our own people telling us how "nappy" our head is, and mamas popping us in the neck for crying when all that tugging at our strong hair/tender scalps gets to hurting, and watching TV and magazine ads celebrate little brown girls with fine, loosely-curled, "other" hair. Brought up to believe this hair is a chore and a burden.

And so I wash and condition and massage and mix elixirs and spray and oil and twist and part and braid. And I don't complain. At least not to my girls. Because I want—need!—them to know that their hair is beautiful just the way it is, no matter what other people think about it, no matter how many think it should be "tamed."

Beautiful indeed. Every. Single. Strand. —*NOVEMBER 2009*

CHAPTER 36

Lessons on Touching, Rocking, and Loving Kinks & Curls

S HE WAS IN HER EARLY 30s when she passed away from complications associated with diabetes and we were all in deep mourning as we sat in her mother's living room, waiting for the limousine that would drive us to her farewell. Memories were exchanged. There were tears, of course. And then all attention fell on us. Specifically, my baby daughter, barely two years old, and her hair.

"You need to comb that stuff," one auntie sniffed, looking with great disdain at my Lila's Afro. My attempts at justifying why I thought it better to keep her hair moisturized and let it just do what it do were met with side-eyes and teeth-sucking from the roomful of old southern black ladies. "Put it in some pigtails or press it or something. Tame it is what you need to do."

The one thing as certain as death? Black women sitting around judging another sistah's hair. I mean, we were on our way to a funeral, for goodness' sake, and there they were, discussing the merits of snatching my kid's hair into a style they thought was more acceptable than the one that celebrated the way it grew out of her head.

Back then, in the early 2000s, this was standard conversation anywhere I or my daughters wore our naturals around black folk; the stares, the side-eyes, the "why's," the questions about "appropriateness"—it was never-ending back then, when wearing your hair in an Afro, braids, twists, Bantu knots, locs or any other natural hairstyle was much less the norm than it is today. I had my reasons for going natural, the biggest one being that my oldest daughter, Mari, nearly scalped herself cutting off her twists so that she could have straight, blonde hair like one of her little classmates.

She was three.

I nearly died a thousand deaths.

Rather than stage a Drop Squad-styled/Happy To Be Nappy intervention on my baby, I went natural to prove to both my brown girls that their kinky, curly hair was more beautiful to me than anything I could buy in a Korean beauty supply store. I needed my babies to know that, and there wasn't a day that passed by that my husband Nick and I didn't tell them how spectacular their hair was—soft like cotton candy, strong enough to break a comb, shinier than a new penny, perfect for parting and a million little twists and a bunch of beads swinging and clacking in the wind. Each of these things I'd whisper into their chocolate little ears as my fingers weaved fantastic styles through their hair. And soon enough, I was satisfied that both Mari and her little sister were happy being exactly who they are: beautiful bundles of chocolate goodness with kinky black girl hair.

And the more they fell in love with their hair, the more confident they grew in rocking their styles. And the more confident they were, the more adoration they got for looking delicious— particularly from their white friends and their moms. That latter part was always such a shock to me. After all, I'd spent years fighting my own people on the merits of rocking natural hair and keeping my daughters natural, too. The idea that the styles I spent upwards of four hours creating in my daughters' heads were complimented and adored by anyone, let alone white girls was . . . interesting.

Of course, the questions were inevitable: how long did it take to get her hair like that? Where did you learn how to cornrow? Does it hurt? Do you take it down every night? How does it stay that way? And for how long? Can I touch it?

I know, I know—I was supposed to pause on all of that, right? After all, my girls aren't museum exhibits, they're not animals in a petting zoo. And, as recounted in a CNN report late last year, there's all kinds of history and baggage that bubbles to the surface when white folk try to touch black women's hair.

Thing is, the questions and the touching doesn't offend me in the least. Don't get it twisted: you better ask first, or risk drawing back a nub. Both my girls understand and will tell you with a quickness that their hair is a part of their body and not a living soul has the right to touch them in any way without their express permission. But what, exactly, is the harm in answering questions from people who genuinely just want to know the answer? Or who have never seen a thick head of kinky hair up close or never felt the glory of a thick, beautiful mane of black girl hair between their fingertips?

Mari's friends really dig her locs, notice when they're freshly palm-rolled and scented with rose-water, rosemary, and grapefruit oil, and love helping her tie them into cute styles. Lila's friends get a kick out of loosening and redoing her twists and trying to duplicate the intricate parts and cornrows in their dolls' hair.

Granted, their love of my daughters' hair grew out of curiosity at first, but now, their playing in each other's hair is no different from them painting each other's toes or pretending to put makeup on each other's faces or playing dress-up. Play in each other's hair is what girls do. Especially if they're friends and they're familiar with each other and they are comfortable in each other's space. This doesn't happen if you're slapping peoples' hands away and telling them that touching your hair is akin to slave masters examining black bodies on the auction block circa 1836. Around our way, it's just not that deep.

In fact, I like to think that their asking—and yes, touching—teaches a very useful lesson about black girl beauty. That in a world where we have "researchers" trying to scientifically prove that black women are ugly, natural, kinky, curly black girl hair is lovely and worthy of celebration. That it matters.

That it is something beautiful—exactly the way it grows out of our heads. —*AUGUST 2012*

CHAPTER 37

Natural Hair Wars

F OR WEEKS, my mother was laid up in a hospital bed with a serious back injury, and so it was on my dad, the quintessential jack-of-all-trades, to pick up the mom slack—fix dinner, do laundry, and check homework between all of his "Dad-type" responsibilities, like making sure the car had oil and the lawn was mowed. All of the mom stuff, Daddy did reasonably well, considering. I mean, he tended to lean a little bit too hard on his go-to dish of smothered liver and mashed potatoes—but my brother and I, we weren't hungry. And he ruined a few loads of laundry by adding bleach to my mom's good chocolate brown towels and a red shirt or two in the whites—but my brother and I, we weren't naked, so that was a good thing, too.

Still, when it came to styling my hair, let's just say my Daddy, bless his heart, was useless. See, my mother and I had a standing Saturday night appointment with a tub of hair grease and a hot comb, and weekdays, it was her duty to make sure I didn't look like Wild Thang climbing onto the school bus. Daddy? He didn't know nothin' 'bout no hot combs and hair grease or hair baubles and barrettes or natural black girl hair—nothing, that is, except that it should look pretty and be anything but nappy. And so only a few days into his Mr. Mom routine, his reasonably cute 12-year-old daughter was beginning to look embarrassingly unkempt.

For my sake and his sanity, he did what any self-respecting dad with little money and even less hairstyling skills would do:

he slapped a jheri curl in my hair. One of those generic, style-at-home jheri curls, with the "easy-to-follow" directions on the box—directions that promised low-maintenance and glamour style.

Right.

Let's just say that maintenance wasn't exactly low (what with all the spraying I had to do to make my style look more "curl" than Afro), and glamour was definitely not high (considering that there was never enough of the uber-expensive spray to make my style look more "curl" than Afro).

Indeed, I like to refer to this time in my life as the beginning of Hair Wars. It was a dark and scary time in which I spent many a morning dreading going to school, and evenings begging my dad to just let me cut my hair and start anew. But Daddy wasn't having it. A southern gentleman to the core, he believed with all his heart that hair is sacred—especially if it brushes the shoulders and blows in the wind. He would never let any girlchild of his cut her "crown and glory"—even if it was stringy, drippy, Afro mess.

His Long Hair by Any Means Necessary edict continued through my high school years—the man would escort me to my hair appointments and literally issue all manner of threat to my stylist if she dared cut my hair—and even into college, when he'd make quick work of giving a disapproving eye if my hair wasn't "done" or, heaven forbid, I wore an African wrap around my head. Mostly, I wore my hair like Daddy preferred because, well, he's my Dad and what daughter doesn't want the approval of the first man she's ever loved—the first to ever love her back? Daddy had very few conditions for his love; all he required was that I do my best, try my hardest, stay out of trouble, and wear my hair straight.

It wasn't until I got pregnant with my second daughter—I was well into my 30s—that I stopped being concerned about my Dad's approval of my hairstyles and did what I wanted to do for years: go natural. Maybe because there was more physical distance between us—he lived in New York, a state away from my New Jersey home. Maybe because I'd become the mom of two girls of my own, whose natural, kinky, curly hair was more beautiful to me than anything I could buy in a box.

I needed my babies to know that, too—that the hair that grows out of their heads is spectacular just the way it is. Even if their Papa didn't agree. So natural I went.

All these years later, I'm happy to say my dad doesn't give me a hard time when I and my girls come bouncing into his house, our hair twisted or loc'd or happily, gloriously kinky and natural (though I do take extra care to make sure that it looks super nice and well-groomed). Maybe we can attribute this to old age—the man is just trying to get through the gates, you know? He's got more important things to fret over. Plus, he moved back to that same southern town where, as a youngster, he learned that a woman's "crown and glory" was always straight, only to find that women were now embracing locs and Afros as much as they previously had embraced straight hair made so with the use of chemicals.

Whatever his reasoning, I'm just happy that I can walk into his house relaxed and happy to be me—and that my father is, finally, happy with this, too. —*SEPTEMBER 2014*

CHAPTER 38

A Teen Struggles to Rock Her Locs Proudly, Courageously

I WENT #TEAMNATURAL with a very specific intention: to show and prove to my daughter, Mari, that she should be proud of her hair exactly how it grows out of her head. And for more than 14 years, I've lovingly tended to every curl, kink, and tendril on her scalp, speaking power and strength into them and her, with a mother's hope that by modeling, praising, and encouraging her natural journey, she would be all good. That each of these things would be enough.

I underestimated, though, the power of other—other images of black women in the spotlight, rocking weaves like it's some kind of superpower, other thoughts in her head about what it means to be a 14-year-old African American girl with locs among a cadre of friends with relaxed, straight hair, and boys other than her daddy and her brother, who have their own warped ideas of what constitutes beauty. And I found out only recently and quite by surprise that the girl just isn't feeling her natural hair. Not like I'd hoped she would.

In other words, when it comes to rocking her natural hair with confidence, she struggles. And because she struggles, I struggle, too.

Recently, I found this poem among the many poems and personal essays she penned for school last year. It is called, "My Hair," and in it, Mari is curious, defiant, fierce. Vulnerable. Her piece led us to a new conversation about our natural hair, one that is decidedly deeper than the many we've had up until now. More grown up.

I am grateful for the conversation.

And scared to death of it.

Mari gave me permission to share her poem with the *MyBrownBaby* readers. I hope you see the beauty in her words and that they, too, give you fuel for conversations about hair in your own homes with your own children.

MY HAIR
By MARI CHILES

Nappy.
A derogatory term that rings in the ears
of every black girl
that wears her hair the way it grows out of her head.
Criticism after criticism tumbling out of the mouths
of those that the corrupt society has captured.
Dreams being crumpled up and thrown into the trashcan
of pointless ideas
just because she has dreadlocks falling down her
        shoulders.
And they wonder why I would rather tug at each strand
        so that
I could get it straightened
instead of wearing it
how it is.
See, I want to turn things around.
Bend it, twist it, cut it, so that it can be even again.
Straighten things out so that they can be the way they
        should be.
Because you people have obviously gotten it all wrong!

Is it okay for a little black girl to grow up believing that
    her real hair
isn't good enough?
Is it okay for her mother to drown her hair in perms and
    relaxers
so that her natural hair won't ever be the same?
Is it really okay for a black woman to be turned down from
    a job
just because she has dreadlocks hanging down her back
no matter how intelligent she is?
Over the years
even I was made to believe it's okay.
5th grade
Hair salon chair
Excited
There I sat as she
tugged on my hair, twisting it like my mom always did
but this time, it remaining
filling out to form locks
Remaining
Like the damages done to a little black girl's Afro
after it is drenched with hair altering chemicals.
Remaining like the "nappy" headed stereotypes and
    ideas
that aren't even true
but still filter their way down into my head
making me question my own hair.
Put me in a group of black girls my own age
and I will probably be one with very few others
that actually have natural hair.
I stand out.
But is that good?
I search deep down into my mind

trying to figure out if I have the guts to stand out
in a society where natural black girl hair is a "no-no"
while struggling to find the courage
to tell my mother
that I want
to take
my dreadlocks
out.
Trying to surpass the stereotypes and assumptions
that people make is hard.
Trying to find the courage to do it is even harder.

—*AUGUST 2013*

CHAPTER 39

Who Needs White Celebrities to Say Locs Are Beautiful When WE Can?

H ERE'S THE THING: despite all the noise and the "what she say?" and the snatching of edges and the Change.org petitions and Twitter apologies and whatnot, the fact still remains that Giuliana Rancic said something incredibly dumb about teen actress Zendaya's hair and really, we're the fools for getting all bent out of shape about it.

In a post-Academy Awards segment on her show, *Fashion Police*, Rancic and her co-hosts were critiquing former Disney star Zendaya's red carpet Oscar outfit when Rancic joked that she thought Zendaya's hair, styled in faux locs, made the 18-year-old look like she "smelled of patchouli oil and weed." Stereotype much?

Mind you, when Rancic critiqued Kylie Jenner's faux locs on an earlier show, they were "cool" and "edgy" on the white girl. But Lord, let a young black woman (yes, Zendaya is biracial but has publicly identified as black) wear a hairstyle honoring the way our hair grows out of our heads and, well, all that "cool" and "edgy" takes a backseat to confusion and disgust.

Not to worry: Zendaya got Rancic together real quick on Twitter, where she posted a statement calling Rancic's racially loaded comments "ignorant slurs" that were "pure disrespect" not only to her but to the scores of loc-rockers who proudly wear the style, sans weed smoke and 125th St. oils, including her daddy, brother, best friend, and cousins, plus a league of black intelligentsia that includes everyone from award-winning *Selma* director Ava DuVernay and Grammy Award-winning songstress Ledisi to author Terry McMillan and a grip of Harvard professors.

"There is already harsh criticism of African American hair in society without the help of ignorant people who choose to judge others based on the curl of their hair," Zendaya wrote. "My wearing my hair in locs on an Oscar red carpet was to showcase them in a positive light, to remind people of color that our hair is good enough."

Zendaya's response showed far more class and restraint than some think Rancic deserved, believe that. Folks are all over the innanets, acting like they're ready to toss the reality show star's head on the grill and serve it with a platter of plantain and rice and peas. And the brouhaha was covered on TV, websites, radio shows, and blogs with the importance of, like, Watergate, the Kennedy assassination, and the capture of Osama Bin Laden.

I can agree that the madness that flew out of Rancic's mouth was in poor taste—fighting words, certainly, in the *MyBrownBaby* household, where natural hair rules and both my older daughter and I proudly wear locs along with everyone from my in-laws and nephew to a few of my best friends. But you know what? This is what Rancic, Kathy Griffin and the rest of the *Fashion Police* talking heads do: they flash pictures of celebrities on a screen, tear them down from head to toe with tasteless disses they think pass as critical commentary and "comedy," and then collect checks for the trouble while mainstream media hails them as arbiters of fashion and taste.

But that's what mainstream media does. In the back rooms of magazines, TV shows, and the like, mostly lily-white staffs create the beauty standards and celebrate those who meet their limited, nonsensical, impossible-to-meet, homogenous criteria. But this is not what *we* do. We black folk know better than to buy into the foolishness that finds its way to the covers of white beauty and fashion mags, that gets celebrated on white blogs and in commercials, that gets critiqued on dumbass shows like *Fashion Police*. Sure, decision-makers have their "pets" of color—Lupita, Kerry, JLo—but, for the most part, they spend an inordinate amount of time ignoring the shit out of all things blackety black, and no amount of think pieces, hashtag campaigns, and online petitions is going to ever change that. Simply put: Rancic let all that anti-locs/natural hair judgment spew out of her mouth because she knows nothing about black hair politics, doesn't give a rat's hairy patootie about it, and, despite her initial (non) apology and a more in-depth on-air mea culpa, probably isn't interested in locs or natural hair on black women and will never be required to talk about either ever again.

And why would we want her to? Neither she nor her mainstream beauty/fashion media cohorts will ever truly "get" us. Not like *Essence* does. Not like Afrobella and The Curvy Fashionista and Yes She Slays and Tia Williams and The Style and Beauty Doctor do. Not like your mama and your aunties and your sisters and fly best friends do. Who needs Rancic's negative, clueless, tragic gaze when we know we know better?

Now, I came to this understanding a long time ago, but you know who solidified this logic for me? My girlpie, Mari. I called myself trying to help her understand and digest fashion by picking up copies of *Teen Vogue* and *Lucky* for her at the grocery checkout line. My thinking: she's a growing teen and she's going to need to know about the fashion and beauty trends of kids her age as she starts thinking about her own sense of style, so let me grab what appeals to teens and get it into her hands.

Wrong move.

I noticed about four months in that the magazines were just laying around the house, completely unread. An inquiry into why she wasn't paying them any kind of mind yielded this nugget: "There's nothing in there for me."

That was my "duh" moment. Of course she didn't see herself in there. No locs. Little chocolate skin. No curves. No Hip Hop. No celebration of us. No black teen stars. No stories about the things she thinks about as a black teen in America. Zero flavor. Mari wasn't about to waste her time on that foolishness.

And we shouldn't either. Go off on Rancic for her ignorant remarks, sure, but put more of that passion into supporting those of us who celebrate us without apology. Who love us unconditionally. Who think we are unapologetically beautiful, exactly the way we are. —*FEBRUARY 2015*

Parenting Beyond Stereotypes

CHAPTER 40

The Tiger Mom Effect

I DON'T KNOW—maybe her balls were just hanging low that day. How else to explain how easily it rolled off her tongue? "You're not like all the other black men. You go to work and pay your bills. You're not lazy like the rest of them."

That was the pearl that Ms. Pearl, our former nanny, dropped on Nick one cold winter morning, as he stooped down to kiss our Mari and rub my pregnant belly and make his way to his job as the editor-in-chief of a travel magazine. Surely, Nick's back stiffened. I know mine did.

Silence clung to the air between us like a nor'easter—thick and frigid and heavy and gray. This sweet little old Guyanese lady, charged with caring for my African American girlpie while we, the married, loving, accomplished parents toiled away our day earning cash to pay the mortgage and the nanny's salary, had managed to, in one breath, slap the crap out of us (and black people in general) with insult, stereotype and backhanded praise. Like, how do you even begin to respond to a "you're not like the rest of them" statement and then leave your baby in your insulter's care? And if she was willing to say that to the faces of her employers, what other stereotypes—certainly more bruising in their insult—did Ms. Pearl have tucked away in the recesses of her brain? And how much of it seeped out of her mouth when we weren't around—in earshot of our impressionable little black girl?

Let's just say that Ms. Pearl's services ended soon thereafter.

Thing is, I'm almost 2,000 percent sure that firing her didn't change her perception of black Americans—or Americans in general. In our country for only a few years, she'd had some pretty clear perceptions about Americans—no doubt formed in her own country and bolstered by her tenuous surroundings in a not-so-nice part of Newark, New Jersey, the six o'clock news, and one-too-many episodes of *Maury Povich* and *Cops*. Americans in general (and, apparently, black folk in particular), she repeatedly stated in her trill Guyanese accent, are lazy, coddle their bratty children, complain about everything, and regularly squander the vast opportunities that this country has to offer.

This is a sentiment that has legs amongst far too many immigrants—people who, armed with their own cultural mores and notions of what is good and right and necessary to succeed, come to America in pursuit of the American dream, even as they shun the people who created and live it. I've heard Ms. Pearl's words repeatedly, in different accents, in a myriad of situations, from African and Jamaican and Indian and Latino and European friends and strangers alike. And this was certainly my takeaway after reading the pure and utter insults advanced in a *Wall Street Journal* excerpt of Amy Chua's book, *Battle Hymn of the Tiger Mother*.

In it, Chua suggests that Asian children are academically, culturally, and mentally superior to American children because their mothers are strict, no-nonsense parents who demand—and get—obedience and perfection from their kids, even if they have to use punishment, excoriation, and shame to get it. American children, she compares, stay losing because, well, we moms coddle and worry and fret over our children's "feelings" and let our kids "give up" easily because we American moms are quitters—too lazy to demand better.

What most disgusts me about Chua—and, by extension, Ms. Pearl—is this utter willingness to trade in stereotypes of her own people to make herself feel superior, all the while serving on a platter every juicy stereotype she can muster to put down Americans. Be clear: there is some truth to stereotypes. By definition, they are oversimplified, standardized images of a people. Emphasis needs to be placed, though, on the word *oversimplified*, whether that stereotype is meant to be positive or negative.

To have Ms. Pearl tell it, for instance, Guyanese people are hardworking, intelligent people whose strict childrearing tactics produce respectful, hardworking, intelligent children. Never mind that Ms. Pearl's grown, 30-something daughter laid around in her pajamas all day while her mother worked, or that Ms. Pearl's 17-year-old granddaughter, who'd made Ms. Pearl a great-grandmother at just 52, lived on public assistance and roused from her slumber only to eat, sleep, crap, and watch *Jerry Springer*. It would be foul of me to say this is the condition of Guyanese people. Particularly because I'm sure that in Guyanese and Guyanese-American homes, there are people who are respectful and hardworking and intelligent, as well as people who are brash, lazy, and dumb.

The same can be said for the Chinese. I mean, I'm glad that Chua cheerleads for her people and whatnot, but there are a BILLION people in China. And I can promise you, not all of the kids there are concert-level pianists with 4.2 grade point averages who kick ass on standardized tests—even if the cultural norm there is for moms to berate and belittle their children into succeeding.

Still, that superior stereotype of the uber smart and talented and perfect Asian (and African and Caribbean and Indian and insert-your immigrant-of-choice here) child plays big here in America, without any recognition by Chua or anyone else that these kids are the children of immigrants—people who, for whatever reason, found the gumption and wherewithal and mettle to bring their families to this, our vast land of opportunity, to find better lives for themselves—to better their families. And that takes some balls. The same kind of balls that I'm guessing you can find in any community of people—yes, even American ones—hell-bent on winning and making sure their children do, too.

I see the proof of this up close every year around this time. My husband interviews prospective students for his alma mater, Yale—has for more than 20 years. Kids apply, the college farms them out to alumni for interviews that will determine whether they're Yale material, and a handful of them wind up on my living room couch, shaking and nervous and praying to sweet baby Jesus/Buddha/Allah/Jehovah/whatever-God-they-pray-to that they can impress my husband—a beautiful, brilliant, successful black man whose parents did NOT have to beat up and yell at and berate and humiliate and threaten their son in order for him to succeed—enough to talk their way into one of the top colleges in the world. And I promise you, those students are not all Asian.

They are the children of white blue-collar workers whose modest homes butt up against trailer parks in neighborhoods where Walmart is the fancy store. They are the children of Mexicans, whose hardworking parents toil under America's harsh anti-immigration (read: anti-Mexican) glare, but still insist that their children press on, do their best and succeed—prove wrong everyone lined up against their country and culture and language. They are the children of Ghanaians and Jamaicans and Nigerians and Trinidadians who live in grand houses in expensive neighborhoods, paid for with the salaries afforded doctors and lawyers and entrepreneurs who found success here in the United States when there was none to be had in their own countries. They are the children of African American single moms struggling to make ends meet, and black parents who, too, are Yale and Harvard alums with impressive titles and homes and bank accounts.

They are the children of families who parented in all kinds of ways—with too much discipline and not enough, with hugging and with slapping, with encouragement and ridicule, with

Helicopter Parent-style attention and hands-off, Free Range Kids-style parenting.

None of these kids are better than the other. None of them worse. They're just students who, because of their circumstances or despite them, managed to get what they think they need to be the people they think they want to become. And honestly, I don't think that's somehow superior to, say, the kids who skip college altogether and become plumbers and electricians and hairdressers and store clerks and nannies.

No matter their mama's parenting style, each of them is simply, beautifully, perfectly human. —*JANUARY 2011*

CHAPTER 41

The Duality of African American Life

I T'S NOT THAT THE GIRLPIES haven't ever been anywhere nice: they've sunbathed on the beaches of Martha's Vineyard, sipped lemonade on the porches of the Gullah on Sapelo Island, wrapped themselves in thick blankets during a horse-drawn carriage through Central Park and, my God, strolled the gardens of Versailles. They are the children of intelligent, curious people who have been blessed with the ability to work hard and save up for meaningful vacations and experiences and so where we go, Mari and Lila go, and what we find interesting, they do, too.

But this past weekend, our travels were different. More purposeful. I treated my daughters to a meal at one of the fanciest restaurants in town, fulfilling a promise I made to them earlier this summer. They are foodies—we watch and root for our favorites on Bravo's *Top Chef* like dudes do their favorite quarterbacks on *Monday Night Football* and my ladies love a well-cooked meal— so the thought of a fine meal prepared by a culinary star in Atlanta had the two of them downright giddy.

The experience did not disappoint: it made my heart swell to see my daughters enjoy fine dining—to know, for sure, what it feels like to dress beautifully for dinner, and have a gentleman pull out their chairs and gently place a cloth napkin on their lap, and to order from a menu featuring braised octopus and roasted duck and sunchoke and rabbit and other eclectic delicacies that they won't get on even the most inspired nights at our dinner table.

And I couldn't have been more proud of them; they were adventurous with their meal choices, minded their manners beautifully, and were genuinely excited as they took in all around them—the décor, the ambience, the respect they got from the waitstaff, how fancy they felt ordering from a menu devoid of burgers and chicken fingers and other kid-friendly fare. No matter that they are wont to act like banshees at our dinner table at home, they were perfect ladies where it counted.

And when we toasted, I made sure they understood—really understood—what our fancy dinner date was all about. For Nick, taking Mari and Lila out was so that they wouldn't be impressed by some boy who'll surely come along and think spending a lot of money on a date is pretty much all he'll need to do to get into our daughters', shall we say, good graces. For me, taking my daughters to dinner was about making sure that they understand that when you work hard, it's important to celebrate a job well done with a well-earned treat for yourself—something that extends far beyond the bills and the worry and the politicking and the tricking that comes with making a couple dollars.

It was Mari, though, whose eyes were opened widest by the experience. Halfway through the appetizers, I noticed her looking—saw the expression on her face as she peeped first, the patrons at our neighboring tables, and then the tables beyond them, too, and then at the waitstaff and the men who cleared our plates and neatened our tables between courses.

"I see you looking," I said when her wandering eyes finally landed on mine. "What do you see?"

"Everyone here is white," she said simply. "We're the only ones."

"And what of the waiters?" I inquired.

"All of them are white, and the ladies at the front door were white and the people cleaning the dishes are Indian and Asian," she said.

Precisely.

We didn't shy away from the conversation; our daughters needed to understand the goodness and the sadness all rolled up in this particular experience—how awesome it was that we had the means on this particular night to enjoy this gustatory experience, but how maddening it is that more of us simply cannot, and how infuriating it is, too, that right here in the middle of a black city with a collection of elite Negroes doing amazing things in business and entertainment, clearly someone had made an executive decision that pretty blondes should be at the door and young white men should serve and get all the tips and "The Others" should clean and the black folk need not bother coming up in there for anything at all.

It was a sociological lesson we weren't intending on having this weekend for our chocolate, smart, accomplished girlpies, but one we had nonetheless. The duality of worlds. Our places in it. The pleasure and the pain that dances all up and between the experiences—all at once sweet and bitter and ugly and beautiful.

This will be their lives.

We will prepare them the best we know how.

The souls of black folk. —*NOVEMBER 2013*

CHAPTER 42

200 Words on Racism, Black Families, and Our Inalienable Right to Just . . . Be

T HERE IS A HOUSE in a nice neighborhood in a good school district in a chocolate city devoid of soul. The black-hand-side kinda soul, I mean. Apparently, there is no room for such things in Atlanta, where old aunties' houses are now fried, dyed, and fully gentrified by that new "new" Atlanta that wants its homes and schools and stores and neighborhoods lily. Damn our money. Damn our education. Damn our picture-perfect, picket-fence-ready family. Go on, git. Our kind is not wanted here. There is no rope. There is no tree. But it feels like a lynching nonetheless. Trying to keep that strongface, y'all. For the sake of my babies. For the sake of my sanity. But really, I'm feeling like a room without a roof. But not in a Pharrell "'cause I'm happy" kinda way. We just want a nice, safe place to lay our heads. A good school for the girl-pies. Some grass to play on and a grocery store stocked with healthy food. Does black skin really negate these things? In 2014, no less? Makes me wanna holler, throw up both my hands. And put a clip in mama's gun. Why can't we ever just . . . be? *—JUNE 2015*

CHAPTER 43

Just Say NO to the Stereotyping of African American Parents and Other Moms and Dads of Color

L IKE, WHAT KID doesn't dig the park? Mari loved the slide, you know? And the monkey bars. And especially when I pushed her on the swing. Her plea was stickier and sweeter and more delicious than a cherry pop: *Higher, mommy! Higher! I want to kiss the sky* . . .

I delighted in watching my baby jump and twirl and fly and pucker up toward the sunshine. Her happiness was infectious. But my hate for the park was equally passionate—searing. Particularly when visits with my then two-year-old daughter fell outside of official playgroup playdates and it was just me and the kid and my swollen, pregnant belly and my elephant ankles and those eyes—those evil, prying, judgmental, better-than-thou eyes that, in a single glance, would betray the conspiratorial conversations The Playground Mafia dug into when they saw me and my chocolate beauty trotting up the walkway.

It never failed; I always got the distinct impression that neither my baby nor I was welcome there. It was all up in the icy glares. The side-eyes and whispers whenever I smiled in their direction or tried to make small talk. The rolling cloud of sensible shoes and mom jeans and crocheted sweaters that always seemed to stampede toward The Children of The Playground Mafia whenever my baby girl penetrated their invisible barrier bubbles.

Always—always—I'd act like it didn't matter. For my baby's sake. But on the walk home, I'd stew and silently wonder what, exactly, ran through their minds—their little, teeny-weeny minds—when they saw me. Maybe they thought I was the nanny—untouchable and unworthy of conversation (unless they were looking for a new one, and then I'd get a fresh "family" card pressed into my palm. True story). Maybe they thought I'd hitched a ride from nearby Newark, New Jersey, so that my kid could play in the "good" park. Maybe they thought I was a teenage mom, slumming off the system, popping out babies and intent on scaring all the good, hardworking white people at the park while I waited for their tax dollars to convert into my welfare check.

After a while, I stopped wasting precious brain matter trying to comprehend why The Playground Mafia acted the way they did to my daughter and me. It became painfully clear relatively quickly that it would never occur to them that I was a neighbor, who, while on maternity leave from a high-paying magazine gig, frequented my neighborhood park to escape endless reruns of *Teletubbies* and *The Wiggles* back at my more than half-million-dollar home, four blocks away.

It would never occur to them that I always bought my shrimp and salmon and whiting at the local fish market and the French bread with the wickedly crusty crust from the local bakery and that my neighbors literally held vigil outside my house on block party afternoons, waiting to dig into my huge basket of fried chicken, hot and sweet.

It would never occur to them that I adored George Clooney and collecting art and throwing dinner parties and writing—that I was interesting and funny and smart and madly in love with my husband and growing family.

That I could love.

And was loved.

This, apparently, is not the stuff black folk are made of—at least not in the minds of some suburban white moms. Exhibit A is this blog post, written by a white mom blogger who got all freaked out when her son struck up an afternoon playground friendship with the son of a man she surmised was a "gang member":

> "How did you KNOW he was a gang member?" I can hear you asking from behind your computer monitor. I'll admit, I'm not exactly up on my "Signs Your Child's Friend's Dad Is A Gang Member" literature. Let's just say it seemed likely. There was the prison number tattooed on his neck, for example. And the cryptic, graffiti-like tattoos all over his arms. And the white tank top. And the baggy jeans. And the bandana. And the unlaced shoes. And the baseball cap worn sideways. If he wasn't a gang member, he definitely wanted people to think he was.

The writer goes on to chronicle how, even though the "gang member" tried to strike up a conversation with her—you know, what normal human beings tend to do when other human beings are around and the kids are playing together—her side of the talking stalled because she wasn't "well-versed in gang member icebreakers" and she couldn't think of anything to say to him beyond, "When's the little guy's initiation?"

Later, when the two scooped up their sons and tossed each other a "see ya," the blogger considers telling the "gang member" how much she enjoyed the gang movie *Colors*, and silently wishes she had a camera to document the occasion so that years later, she could reminisce with her son about "that gang member" who pushed him on the swing. "Such a *nice* gang member . . ." she imagined she would say to her son as they flipped through their scrapbook of memories.

She and the posse in her comments section thought the blog post was humorous.

Laughing yet?

I'm not.

That post, penned by a well-respected blogger who was named a runner-up Must-Read Mom by *Parenting* and BlogHer, hurt me to the core. Because it was offensive. Insulting. Condescending. And stupid. For me and a lot of other moms of color who read it, including my blog friend Elita Kalma of the breastfeeding site *Blacktating*, who showed me the blog post, it was a painful reminder of the slights and stereotypes we face down every day, all day when we find ourselves amongst The Playground Mafia; it took me right back to that park in New Jersey, where I went looking for friendship and found only impudence—the mental version of white women clutching their purses and locking their car doors when black people come walking by.

Trust me when I tell you, this is no laughing matter to me as a woman, as an African American, or as a mother, particularly when I know stereotypes such as these can make people see what they *want* to see, rather than *who we are*. And real talk? It can get black folk killed.

It's not a game.

It seems, too, that in this age, when white suburban kids are trying to look like Lil Wayne and black urban kids are swimming in preppy gear and honor roll students like my 6' 1", 270 pound son might just find himself at the park with his pants sagging and his football player biceps bulging, pushing his little sisters on the swings, it's kinda foolish to assume anything about anybody based on what they're wearing on their backs.

But for kicks and giggles, let's just say that the man she met in the park was a gang member. Does such a distinction preclude him from being interesting? Intelligent? Articulate? Human? Certainly, these characteristics aren't the exclusive preserve of middle class white moms. And Mr. "Gang Member" tried to hold a conversation with someone who wasn't big enough, savvy enough, smart enough, loving enough, and open-minded enough to reciprocate, which tells me a lot more about him than his bandana ever would.

For sure, I'd take the "gang member"—tats, bandanas, slouchy pants and all—any day of the damn week before I'd subject myself to the tyranny of assumption advanced by this blogger and The Playground Mafia. And I've already conjured up in my mind how many deaths ol' girl will die the day her son comes home with his "jail number" tattooed on his neck, looking very much like our neighbor's son, a white 18-year-old who wears bandanas and wife-beaters and sagging pants and tats all over his skin and who makes our block tremble when he drives by in his Mustang with his rap music blasting, headed for class at a local two-year college. He's a nice boy. You wouldn't know it by the way he dresses, but you would definitely discover it if you bothered to open your mouth and, like, have a conversation with him.

Here's the thing: this mother has the right to make all the assumptions she wants, to ignore all the people she wants—to pass judgment and call names and withhold friendship based on superficial gut reactions. People of color have grown quite used to the middle class white moms who sniff at our presence and make clear with their actions that when it comes to forming relationships, people who don't come from the same place as or who don't look/speak/act like them need not apply. (Please don't get your panties in a bunch: I'm not saying ALL white moms are like this. But I've run into enough in my day to know plenty exist.)

Do me this solid, though: if that's the way you feel, keep it to yourself, m'kay? Better you let me *think* you're an asshole than to open your mouth (or write a blog) and remove all doubt.

—OCTOBER 2010

CHAPTER 44

Evil Black Men

I T WAS SUPPOSED TO BE a simple assignment—a little something to remind the kids about their lesson on adjectives. Magazine and newspaper clippings + lots of glue + fancy descriptives = an easy lesson and the perfect student work display for the parent-teacher conference.

We all drank in the oversized poster boards, we parents patiently waiting in the hallway for our turn with the teacher. Mari pointed lazily at the big navy blue sheet she worked on with her group; there were cars that were "slick" and "fast," desserts that were "tasty," and chairs that were "pretty" and "comfy."

And then there were the postage-stamp-sized newspaper cutouts of young black men, three of them spread out across the paper. Beneath each of them, written in simple, neat black bubble letters was one word: evil.

The hell?

Mari got questioned first: who wrote "evil" under those pictures? And why? Did the story the pictures came from show these boys were criminals? Did you *see* the story? Did you have anything to do with this? Did it occur to you to tell whoever wrote this that this wasn't nice?

I got little more than crickets from the kid. That and a bunch of "I don't knows." So I left her alone. Until, that is, I moved on to the next poster board, and the next one, too. On each poster, there were at least a dozen cutouts of black men glued down and summarily objectified.

Ugly.

Scary.

Bad.

Insolent.

Each adjective, it seemed, was uglier than the last. And each of those ugly words are the ones that first came to mind when the children in my daughter's class—many of whom she calls friends—saw pictures of black men.

This—this was bigger than some random comments, some smart-ass kid who thought it would be funny to say mean things about random people. This was deep-seated stereotyping at its worst—at first blush, the innocent ramblings of 10-year-olds, but, in our eyes, symbolic of a much larger issue: even these children, young as they are, were falling prey to the negative hype that black man = bad.

Blame it on media imagery, pop culture, racism, ignorance, immaturity, naiveté—a combination of all of them. Neither Nick nor I could be sure who or what to blame. What we did know was that when we got our turn to talk to Mari's teacher, we were going to request the posters be removed from the wall and that she consider having a talk with the kids about perceptions, stereotypes, and adjectives that hurt.

This is what Nick and I were discussing (privately, mind you) when a fellow parent burst into our conversation, accusing us of "making a big deal out of nothing" and "trying to find something that's not there."

"What about this picture?" she yelled (literally yelled!), jabbing her finger at a cutout of a football player about to be tackled, holding a football in his strong embrace. Beneath his picture, a student scrawled "sporty." "You both just conveniently ignored that picture!"

Dead. Fish. Eyes.

Now, I'd like to tell you that Nick and I handled this woman with grace—that our conversation was measured and neat and that we had a Kumbaya moment and laced fingers and pinky-sweared better cultural understanding. But er um, yeah—it didn't go down that way. Let's just say it got ugly and voices were raised and accusations were made and, despite my husband's petition for her to "walk in our shoes for a day, a month, a year, a lifetime" before she dared tell us how we should feel about the blatant stereotyping of black men on our children's class work, she just wouldn't acknowledge that something was wrong with those pictures.

Mari's teacher, however, handled our concerns with grace, humility, and a genuine understanding that with kids this age, teachable moments come out of left field and it's on the adults in the room to deal with the situation head-on—to confront and adapt and use them to make children *really think*, instead of shrinking away from them or ignoring them or trying to reason away the obvious to make themselves feel better. The teacher, whom I've loved for many more reasons than just this one instance, allowed herself to see our perspective—how there was no denying that this class-full of 10- and 11-year-olds, a virtual UN of races, backgrounds, religions, and cultures, could internalize negative perceptions of black men.

Heck, even Mari didn't fully comprehend why this was a situation until her father made plain how dangerous it is for people to look at a black man and automatically assume he's bad or ugly or scary. "How wrong would it be if your Daddy were walking down the street, or your brother, or your cousins Miles and Cole, and everyone assumed we all were scary or evil just because of the way we look?" he asked her, before telling her of Amadou Diallo and Sean Bell and Oscar Grant, III, and the long line of black men who were killed after police officers wrongfully assumed they were criminals. Punctuating our points, I showed Mari a blog that, ironically, I'd posted on *MyBrownBaby* earlier that morning about how I feared for her cousin Miles, who will soon look like a man.

Now, my Mari gets it. It's a lesson we weren't quite ready for her to learn, but clearly it was a discussion that needed to be had.

My hope is that my baby isn't the only student who walks with a clearer understanding about adjectives—and the ones that hurt.

—FEBRUARY 2010

CHAPTER 45

The Truth about Black Fathers

THEY WOULD HAVE YOU BELIEVE THIS—that black fathers make the babies and leave the mamas and disappear like the wind, sans a care in the world about their wake's effect. Oh, be clear: there are those who fit the bill. Hearts weep—souls wail in their absence. The scars, ugly, run deep.

But this is only part of the story. Rather, it is not the story—not our sole tale to tell. So many more black fathers square the shoulders and extend the arms and open their hearts and do what is natural and right and beautiful: they love. Hard. Long. Sweetly. Sternly. Thoughtfully.

Beautifully.

I am a witness. My testimony begins in the dark basement of an orphanage, in a crib, where, in a very precise moment, eyes locked and fingers touched and hearts connected, cemented by a man's desire to father a girlchild and a daughter's need for a forever family. It did not matter that my mother did not carry me in her womb. It did not matter that my father did not sow this particular seed. I was his. He was mine. The heavens deemed this so.

My father's love is, all at once, regular and extraordinary—average and heroic. For starters, he was there. He protected us—physically, financially, emotionally, mentally. He worked the overnight shift and hustled side jobs so that we had a roof over our heads and food on the table and clothes on our backs and everything we needed and a few things we wanted, too. He saw to it that we got educated—this man who grew up in the segregated South, where separate and vastly unequal was the law of the land and a solid education was not an option for brown babies like him. He doled out discipline in healthy doses—with great love and the profound knowledge that setting my brother and me straight would go a long way in helping us become better human beings.

It was he who convinced me to write and he who, to this day, I call first when I get another book deal or a story in a national magazine. He keeps all my books and clips on a special shelf in his home—shows them off to family and friends. He is proud of me. Even at 46 years old, I never tire of seeing his chest stick out just a little bit more when he speaks of my work—never tire of him responding to my news of good fortune by saying, "Wow! That's great, doll!"

All of these things my father gave so freely, against the odds. Still does.

They are love.

It's the same kind of love that I see in my own home, with my husband, whose love for and dedication to our daughters and son is so strong, so incredible, so dedicated, so bright, it rivals a thousand stars.

It's the same kind of love I see out on the soccer fields on Saturdays, where little brown girls push the ball up the grass and toward the goal, the wind and their fathers' cheers at their backs.

It's the same kind of love, too, that I see at school functions, where black daddies beam and snap pictures of their children as they sing and present their art and collect their academic certificates for work well done.

Open your eyes at the grocery store, and there is that love, standing over in the fruit section and in the milk aisle, warm and ever-present in the giggles and the "Daddy, can we get that, please?" pleas that tumble from little mouths.

Peek in the barbershops on a Saturday afternoon and that love is sitting on the couch, joking and jonesing and telling stories, with watchful eyes on the little heads getting edged up right.

And it's ever present in church pews on early Sunday mornings, where, with hands raised, black fathers praise their God and show their children, by example, how to do so, too.

The loving, caring, dutiful black father exists. My God, he does. They do. Despite what the black marriage statistics say. Despite what the prison statistics say. Despite what the child support checks look like. Black fathers are capable and do love and care for their babies. It may not be picture-perfect love. It may not always be the way we mothers think black fathers should show their love.

But it's love. And it's there.

It is this on which I choose to meditate on this Father's Day. As the sun dances across the sky and I take this one day out of 365 to celebrate fathers, I choose to give a little air to humanness and imperfection and a pinch of understanding, then focus—really focus—on how love manifests itself in good black fathers. Good black men.

I am a witness.

I know, for sure, I am not the only one. —*JUNE 2015*

CHAPTER 46

The Complexity of Us

I WAS IN THE CAR headed to the Atlanta One Billion Rising rally with Mari and three of her female classmates, singing Prince's "Adore" loud and off-key, when girlpie commandeered the radio dial in search of—what else?—Hip Hop. "I can't believe you turned off Prince," I sniffed. "Since your little friends are in the car, I'll give you that, but please be aware: I'm not feeling Lil Wayne in general and, because of his nasty lyrics about Emmett Till, today I particularly don't like his behind, so he will not be on my radio, please and thank you."

"Wait, huh?" the girls asked, practically in unison. "What did he say?"

Typical. The girls had no clue that one of their generation's most revered rappers was being called out by the civil rights icon's family for comparing sex with the brutal, merciless beating that killed the then-14-year-old Till. For kids, that kind of news never appeals; they nod to the beat, tweet about what Kim Kardashian did on her latest reality show, obsess over Mindless Behavior Instagram posts and ignore that which gets the adults all riled up. Never mind that, though: I was pissed and I wanted them to understand why they should be, too. "I mean, besides constantly making it seem like the only good sex is violent sex, this fool callously used the brutal murder of Emmett Till to describe what he'd like to do to a woman's body. You should be infuriated."

And then I stopped myself short. "Wait: y'all do know who Emmett Till is, right? *Right?*"

And in that moment between my question and their answer, I really had to wonder if, as a black mom in America, I'd failed my children. Because I couldn't be so sure that I'd taught my own African American babies that particular piece of history. I mean, I thought I'd had, but I couldn't be sure that I'd actually sat them down and said, "Emmett Till was dragged out of his bed by a gang of white men who beat him bloody, gouged out his eyes, shot him in the head, and tied him to a cotton gin fan with barbed wire and tossed him to the bottom of the Tallahatchie River for allegedly whistling at a white woman, and his mother's courageous decision to show his battered, broken, bloated body in an open casket funeral for the world to see was the impetus for the civil rights movement."

Be clear: I think I've done a helluva job instilling positive self-esteem in my black girls; though they still have their moments of self-doubt—what girl doesn't?—I'd like to think that surrounding my daughters with black children's books, music, poems, and consistent messages about how intelligent, smart, thoughtful and, yes, beautiful they are has gone a long way in making them understand that no matter anyone else's opinion, they're some *baaaad* little chicks.

But there are some days that I feel like I just haven't done enough when it comes to the nuts and bolts of who we are as a people—that I've become complacent with our history. It's like February rolls around and someone says something nice about Martin Luther King, Jr. and Harriett Tubman and names all the stuff George Washington Carver made out of peanuts and then we drop it all until the next Black History Month comes creaking along.

This is unfair to my babies. And to our people who came before us—who paved the streets with their blood, sweat, tears, and sacrifice so that my daughters and I could really live. And failing to teach our children the importance of those who paved the way creates a breeding ground for the tomfoolery advanced by the likes of Lil Wayne, who would traffic in hurtful, nonsensical metaphors about our heroes simply to shovel his woefully misogynistic rhetoric on young fans too busy nodding to the beat to understand just how blatantly disrespectful he is to our daughters and our sons.

Of course, there are those who are quick to argue that slavery and Emmett Till and Jim Crow are ancient history; consider the outrageous comments US Supreme Court Justice Antonin Scalia made when he suggested, out loud, that the Voting Rights Act—one that people lost limbs, blood, and lives for; one that was tested as recently as last year's presidential election—is a "racial entitlement." And in states like Texas, Tennessee, and Arizona, conservatives are flat-out trying to pretend our history never existed in the first place by either revising it or, in some cases, outright erasing facts about blacks and Mexicans in the United States from their school curriculums. How many times have you heard white folk make the (stupid) argument that they've "never owned any slaves" and therefore shouldn't have to answer to any of the race remnants that continue to fester throughout our land? Post racial? Yeah. Okay. *insert massive side-eye here.*

I don't need their revised, whitewashed history books or their acknowledgement. I only have to look to my father to be reminded how important it is to remember our history and recount it to our children. Once when I appeared on HLN to talk about the one-year anniversary of Trayvon Martin's shooting death, my father called to congratulate me and we ended up talking for hours about his experience as a young black man in the deep South, where segregation ruled, Jim Crow was the law of the land, and an African American teen would have to be mindful to step off the curb and avoid looking a passing white man in the eye, lest he earn himself a trip to jail and a beating—or worse, the business end of a rope and tree limb.

Having a daddy who can recall those days of separate bath-rooms and water fountains and the indignities of being a black man in pre-civil rights era America puts perspective on things, I'll tell you that much. It also reminds me that there simply is no room for letting our babies be ignorant of our history. We must tell them the story of Emmett Till and Medgar Evers. We must tell them about Bloody Sunday and the Four Little Girls. They need to know about Joseph Cinqué and Ebo Landing and the Gullah culture—the one-room schoolhouses and the colored water foun-tains and the department stores that wouldn't let even our chil-dren try on clothes in the fitting rooms, even though they were quick to take our money. We can't stop at Harriet Tubman and Martin Luther King, Jr. and Rosa Parks and those 28 days in the shortest month of the year. Black history is our history.

American history.

And if we don't remember it, talk about it, and pass it on, surely it will die.

More importantly, if we don't teach it to our children, they won't know it—and this will be nobody's fault but our own. Most schools won't be teaching it. Our children are not going to learn it on the television. And they sure as hell won't pick it up in a Lil Wayne lyric. This doesn't mean that our children don't care and aren't interested in learning it. It simply means that we parents are falling down on our jobs when it comes to making sure that our children are up on the history, its context, and what it means to their world today.

I thank goodness that Mari and her fellow students—one African American, two white—knew the story of Emmett Till. Mari told me later that she couldn't remember if I told her about him or if she learned about him in school. I'm grateful that she knew, no matter who taught it to her, but I know that there's a lot more for my daughter to learn. I've got work to do. How about you? —MARCH 2013

CHAPTER 47

Why White Parents Should Teach Their Children about Race

R EALLY, IT WASN'T PLANNED, this cornucopia of color and races and backgrounds and experiences. It was just Mari's birthday party, a tiny affair that involved five beautiful 12-year-old girls with big personalities, lots of shared interests in *Lemonade Mouth* and *Glee* and an affinity for gourmet strawberry cupcakes and painting each other's toes and fingers. Peeping around the corner into the room where this loud, giggly affair was taking place was like gazing at a Benetton ad on helium: lots of colors, lots of cultures, lots of backgrounds, lots of languages, all united, with a sole mission: to have as much giggly sleepover fun at our place as humanly possible.

They weren't focused on their differences, by any stretch. But I noticed and reveled in them—the hysterically gregarious Ethiopian baby girl of the interracial couple from New Orleans; the motor-mouthed and deliciously bubbly daughter of an African American woman and a Mexican dad; the quiet, observant Jamaican-American; the lanky, thoughtful Chinese child of two white southerners; and my baby, 100 percent black Georgia peach by way of NYC. And I couldn't help but to be proud of my Mari for picking the mix, even if it happened only subconsciously.

Oh, she swears she doesn't pick friends by color or culture or background—that she's an equal opportunity friend, so long as you're a nice person and kinda, sorta dig some of the same things she does. We had an interesting discussion about it, the continuation in an ongoing conversation we've been having about differences. About noticing them. And giving them a nod. And appreciating them for what they are. She understands its import—and for that, I'm grateful. But she told me, too, that picking friends according to some arbitrary thing like skin color doesn't rule her choices either—and for that I'm grateful, too.

I've been considering this a lot this week after I logged onto The Twitter and found this tweet from a white mother named Brenda who blogs about her autistic son on her website, *Mama Be Good*:

> @MyBrownBaby If u get a min, would love 2 know what u think. Why should I teach my child about race?

In the tweet, Brenda included a link to a poignant blog post she penned about her delicious son, Jack, who, it seems, has yet to identify people by skin color, and instead focuses on the shape of people's foreheads and the color of their hair to distinguish one person from another. Jack, she wrote, had said a man with the same wrinkleless forehead and dark-colored hair as his dad looked like his father. This, despite that the man is African American and Jack's dad is Caucasian. And in Brenda's opinion, this is a perfectly acceptable way for her son to identify folk because, well, it's no more random than pointing out someone's skin color. She continued:

> Let's just admit it. Race-based identification is arbitrary. So I haven't "taught" Jack about skin color. I haven't labeled people based on their race. I haven't pointed out that people have different skin colors. I'm curious to see if he notices – ever

– but I can't think of a reason, right now, that he needs to know. I can foresee sometime in the future when we're reading history . . . he already knows Lincoln and some things about the Civil War, all to do with the terrifying fact that people died. And, if for some reason, he began acting differently towards people based on their skin color, or wanted to know why others treated people differently based on their skin color, or if he were treated differently because of his skin color, absolutely. Then we'd need a history lesson and a human being lesson.

And, yes, perhaps not teaching him about prejudice is a luxury we can afford simply because we happen to be Caucasian. I recognize the unfairness. I recognize that this lesson has to occur for some children earlier. And it is unfair. Or perhaps we aren't teaching Jack about prejudice right now 'cause we're still working on the basics. Because Jack is diagnosed with autism. Or because we'll be talking about a different kind of prejudice. Because Jack is diagnosed with autism.

But right now, Jack perceives people without bias. We aren't our skin color. We are people.

And foreheads. Apparently.

I promise you this: Brenda's post—and her question—did make me think and stretch and consider the view from her side of the street; her son sounds precious and my God, who would want to sully that innocence?

The truth is, I wish Jack's way was the way of humans—that we all were blissfully unaware of skin color and all the baggage that comes with it and simply identified people by the number of lines on their forehead or the tint of their hair. But we are humans. And sadly, all too many of us grow up and get grown and get our fill of living and experiences and theories and stereotypical messages both overt and subliminal and, whether we really care to admit it or not, we form our ideas and feast on those of others and, quick as a wink, that idealistic innocence flies right on out the window.

In my writings, I've cited studies and books, too, about how well-meaning white parents do their children a huge disservice when they cloak real historical and cultural issues in vague platitudes instead of taking on the topic of race head-on. Exposing white children to books and toys featuring children of color helps give parents a chance to show not just the differences but the commonalities between the races and cultures and why this is an important conversation to have early and often.

Here's the thing: no matter how much white parents think their silence on the matter will help their kids maintain their innocence when it comes to race, the world will work overtime to feed kids the crazy—kind of like what happens when parents refuse to talk to their kid about sex and then he hits the locker room and some boob tells him he can't get a girl pregnant if he pulls out or that he'll grow hair on his hands if his uses them to masturbate or he can't get HIV from oral sex, and then the kid with all the bad info shows up with a baby or an infection. Like sex, skin color will become one of those things that sticks out like a neon target. It will become a very relevant thing. Maybe not for Brenda. Or her sweet Jack. But for plenty more, I assure. And if the discussion doesn't come up in your house until there's a problem, well, the discussion is way too late.

The truth is I don't have the luxury of walking into the room and having my skin color go unnoticed. I don't have the luxury of applying for a job and having it go unnoticed. I don't have the luxury of going to a restaurant or shopping in a store or driving in a well-to-do neighborhood—even my own—and having people see my forehead or the color of my hair or the hue of my eyes instead of my skin. The same goes for my man and my hulking, football-playing son and my two chocolate girlpies and my elderly daddy, who grew up in the segregated South, and my in-laws, who live in a mostly white neighborhood where their son is the only black child in the class and their other son, a sweet 12-year-old kid who couldn't and wouldn't hurt a fly and loves pretty much anyone he comes in contact with, was called the "N" word for nothing more than that his skin is brown. This is the American way.

And seeing as it can't be hidden and I've worked so hard to love my brown skin despite all of the negative storylines/assumptions attached to it, the last thing I and oh so many more who look like me want is to have someone say she doesn't "see" it. I won't speak for all African Americans because we are not a monolith. I will, however, say that a large part of who I am and what I love about myself is rooted to my race and the culture connected to it; my skin is no less a part of me than my limbs, my breath—my heart. I know for sure that I am not alone in my thinking on this. It does not define me, but this brown skin has helped shape me in immeasurable ways. I can say the same is true for my babies, who, even as they are being encouraged not to dwell on color, are being taught that color and culture *are* important—a part of the myriad of things that makes each of us special and different and beautifully human.

And that, along with foreheads and hair color and a cornucopia of giggly little girls with a rainbow of skin colors, cultures, and backgrounds, is worth noticing. —*JUNE 2011*

THEY'LL WEAR THE ARMOR
Black Children and Racism

CHAPTER 48

Guarding My Babies from The "N" Word

I KNOW THEIR DAY is coming. It is as certain as wet rain, as sure as the yellow in the sun.

They are, after all, African American girls in America. Home of the free. Land of the brave. Where a black man is the president, but Confederate flags still snap in the fall winds. It's only a matter of time. Surely, someone will curl that ugly, searing, poisonous word around the tongue and launch it in my babies' direction.

I wonder under what circumstance they'll hear it—if it'll be on the school bus or at the playground. Maybe it'll be a grown-up, too ugly and nasty and cruel to care about how the word will forever sear my children.

I go over and over again in my mind how I'll explain the vitriol—the contempt—that'll surely be heaped on them by some stranger too ignorant/angry/pathetic to see through blinding stereotypes. I see such innocence in my girls' faces; at ages seven and ten, they don't know much about the harsh lessons black children faced over the years right here in our country. Selma. Four Little Girls. Ruby Bridges. Back of the bus. Separate and unequal. Those babies? They wore the armor, see.

But not my babies. This much, to them, is true: the most powerful leader on the planet is a black man with two daughters who look just like them. And in their little worlds, it's not a thing for little black girls to have white friends and Asian friends and Muslim friends, because what really matters is not so much the color of one's skin but the content of their character, the kind of person you are. Their expectations of others are pure.

They can just . . . be.

Without fear.

Even here in Georgia, in the seat of the Confederacy, where just a generation ago, children who looked like them witnessed unspeakable atrocity.

Still, it's hard for me to claim racial progress with a whole heart. My memories won't allow it. See, I've had that word lobbed in my direction way too many times to forget. The first time, I was 11 years old and brand new—the child of southerners who, in integrating a virtually all-white, working-class Long Island neighborhood, thought it more prudent to embrace racial progress than harp on painful pasts. No one had told me that the word was supposed to hurt, and so I didn't sweat it when our neighbor, with whom I enjoyed playing, said it as simple as "pass the salt" or "may I have another slice of apple pie —"My mom said we can't play with niggers, so . . ." he mumbled. I was sadder about the eight-foot fence my neighbor's mother had built around their house and her orders to her children to stay away from me and my brother than some word whose meaning was still tenuous and blurry to kids like us.

The meaning and the sentiment behind it was crystal clear, though, the next time I heard it. I was riding my bike one block over from my parents' house when the daughter of my Girl Scout troop leader shouted out from her front lawn full of friends, "Nigger want a watermelon?" I was 12. I never went back on that block or to another Girl Scouts meeting—not ever. That's how I dealt with that. And years later, when a fellow student barged into my dorm room, shouting about how "the nigger down at the front desk" wouldn't let her in without showing I.D., I was too scared to do anything other than accept her apology. I'd only been on that college campus for about 30 minutes, and the word "nigger" was already ringing in my ears.

I had a few choice words and a couple middle fingers for the people who called me the "N" word once I grew up and got some mettle—for the guy at the CVS who thought he should get to skip the line where I was waiting to buy Pampers for my baby, for the guy in the parking lot of the Best Buy who thought I should pull out into oncoming traffic because he was in a rush, for the angry Puerto Rican who cursed me in Spanish but knew enough English to call me "nigger" after I almost accidentally rear-ended his car trying to avoid hitting a stalled one in my lane.

I remember every . . . last . . . time.

And each incident still makes my blood boil.

Still, as a mother, I'm desperate to let my black butterflies enjoy the innocence—to avoid having to put on the armor just a little while longer. They deserve, at least, that peace.

For now, my beautiful chocolate butterflies deserve to just . . . be. —MAY 2009

CHAPTER 49

Fighting Words: On the "N" Word & My Children's Response to It

I TOLD YOU THIS would happen—said it was as certain as wet rain, as sure as the yellow in the sun. A white child called a black boy very near and dear to our family a "nigger."

The "who did it" and the "whom it got done to" and the specifics on how it all went down aren't for me to tell. Just know that it happened out on the playground during recess after our beloved bested the white boy in a foot race. Upset that he got creamed in a challenge he issued, the white child looked our beloved in the eye and let the most offensive racial slur you can call a black person, punctuated with the "F" bomb for emphasis, fly.

Our beloved, wanting to make absolutely sure he'd heard the boy correctly, asked, "What did you say?" The white boy, wanting to make absolutely sure that there was no confusion about what he said, repeated himself: "f&*#ing nigger."

Know that our beloved put the little foul-mouthed fool in a headlock.

Know that had the playground monitor not broken it up, the little foul-mouthed fool would have gotten his ass kicked.

I've gone over in my mind for years what I would do, how I would respond on the day that someone hurls that ugly, searing word at one of my brown babies. On my most idealistic days, I've assured myself that I would tell my children that it's the other kid who has the problem, not us—that there are sick people in the world who, for whatever reason, will stupidly employ skin color as a reason for disliking, even hating, another human being and will toss out racial epithets because they're too damn weak, dim, and insecure to hurt us in any other meaningful way.

But I wasn't feeling very idealistic that day. And when my Mari got home and the story was recounted, I told her that if any child ever called her a "f&*#ing nigger," she had my permission to knock her dead in the mouth. Because when I'm not Denene Millner the *Parenting* columnist and bestselling author, I'm Denene Millner-Chiles, African American mom of Mari and Lila, two beautiful chocolate pies who deserve and will get their respect. While my parents didn't give me the tools to understand and deal with being called a nigger when I was little, the Chiles girls are very clear on what to do the day it happens to them. Those two words, especially when paired together, are fighting words. Period. And I'm a firm believer that those whose mouths choose to write that particular check better have an ass ready and able to cash it.

Word is bond.

But you know what's most upsetting about this, friends? It's that The Incident happened in a safe place, a space where Nick and I and our beloved's parents send our kids because most parents who send their kids there seem to be forward-thinking, kind, progressive, and tolerant. I'm still prone to believe this. I want to. Need to. But I know for sure, now, that there is immense danger in "safe." Because in "safe," everyone seems to delude themselves into believing that there are no problems, that everything is fine and dandy, that these kinds of things don't need to be held up to the light and examined and dissected and discussed before the one says something crazy to the other and the other forces the one into meting out a Five Knuckle Shuffle out on the playground.

Dig it: I don't know what's in that child's heart—if he truly is a racist, if he's being raised by racists, if his grandfather or his auntie or his neighbors play fast and loose with the "N" word or he heard it in a Lil Wayne song and thought he'd try it out on our beloved. What I do know is that clearly, the boy has had the word on his mind and nobody is talking to him—*really talking to him*—about race and its legacy or the "N" word and its sting in any meaningful way.

This is typical. In their book *Nurture Shock: New Thinking About Children*, authors Po Bronson and Ashley Merryman say that babies as young as six months old judge others based on skin color and that well-meaning parents do their children a huge disservice when they cloak real historical and cultural issues in vague platitudes—"God made all of us," and "Under the skin, we're all the same," and "Everyone is equal"—instead of taking on the topic of race head-on. The authors also point out that, according to a 2007 study of 17,000 families, nonwhite parents are three times more likely to discuss race, while 75 percent of white parents never, or almost never, talk about race. What's worse, they say, is that by the time parents consider their kids "old enough" to dig into the topic, they may have already created divisions of their own.

Which means that while I'm home with my daughters breaking down the nasty particulars of racism and teaching them how to distinguish between people who really like them for them and jerks who don't deserve their awesome, other parents are sending their kids out into the world completely clueless to the fact that yelling "nigger" at a another kid is not only foul, stupid, and racist, but could get your ass beat.

My two cents? It's all of our responsibility—black, white, Latino, Asian, Russian, African, whatever—to raise unbigoted, tolerant, open-minded, empathetic people, and one of the best ways to do this is for us parents, all of us parents, to actually TALK ABOUT RACE in the same way we do naturally about other family values we think important enough to talk to our kids about, like the importance of boys respecting girls, not making fun of fat people and the disabled, being kind to old people and things like that. It's time for all of us to take our heads out of the sand and deal with this—understand that we're not going to live in a better society until we teach our children how to understand and truly care about the people who actually live in it with all of us. Because each time one of us falls down on the job, it impacts everybody.

And really, I'd prefer my kids not have to bust up your kids because you didn't teach him better. Or at all. —*APRIL 2011*

CHAPTER 50

Black Boy Swagger, Black Mom Fear

H E'S 6 FEET, 250-plus pounds, quite imposing next to my 5' 2 frame, and can bench just shy of 300, which means that if he felt like it, he could flick me like a flea. Lucky for me, I'm his stepmother, and at the very least, he withholds his laughter when I crane my neck, fold my arms, put on my mean mug, and tell him, "I can *still* take you."

Out on the football field, though, my 16-year-old son takes no shorts; as a nose tackle, he's charged with taking on two, sometimes three opposing players at a time. This requires an incredible amount of mental fortitude and swagger, both of which my 16-year-old son has in abundance, especially when he's making his way to the line of scrimmage. Take a good hard look at him on the 50-yard line, and it's easy to get it twisted: he looks like an angry, aggressive, big, black jock, a guy who crushes the opponent on the field; and off the field, probably doesn't put much effort into much more than football, girls, and black boy shenanigans.

I don't know if this is what one of his team's assistant coaches had on his mind recently when he called the boy over to take a look at his class schedule. Mazi handed it to him and shifted nervously from foot to foot, his mind on who knows what. I can only guess what he expected to find, but when that coach looked at Mazi's schedule and then back up at Mazi, I could see in his eyes that his perception of who my boy is was completely, forever changed.

See, what that coach wasn't expecting to see was Honors

Physics. Honors Algebra. Advanced Placement Psychology. Honors Language Arts. And Mechanical Drafting, the first in a series of courses that'll put Mazi on firm footing toward becoming an architect. The grades: almost all As and one B. He's number 44 in a class of 546 and still climbing.

The boy is bad—smart as hell, incredibly sweet, helpful when he wants to be, and pretty easy to get along with. We argue the musical merits of Lupe Fiasco, Kanye West, and Rakim, reminisce over our favorite scenes in *Biker Boyz*, discuss on the regular whether he's going to Yale, Harvard, or Princeton, and sometimes he even comes to me in confidence to discuss how to negotiate his tenuous relationships with the cute but fickle little girls he dates.

He is a normal boy.

A brilliant boy.

A college-bound boy.

A sweet boy.

A black boy.

And every time that child leaves this house, I fear that someone will look at him, his size, his skin color, his swagger, and see what they want to see, and not *who Mazi is*. Not a day goes by without us warning him to be respectful, to watch his tone, to be extra vigilant when approaching people in his path. And last week he got his license and bought himself a car with the cash he makes as a lifeguard, which of course means that now when he snatches his keys and heads for the door, I'm a nervous wreck thinking that he's going to get stopped by the cops.

I have good reason to be nervous for him, you know. At the time of writing this piece, three—THREE!—black men had been shot, two killed, by the police within a span of a week. Adolph Grimes, III, 23, was shot 12 times in his back, 14 times total, on New Year's Day as he made his way to a family party in New Orleans; Oscar Grant, 22, was shot by a transit officer while he lay facedown and handcuffed on a train platform; Robbie Tolan, 23, was recovering from gunshot wounds to his liver and lung after being shot in his own driveway by a Houston police officer who accused him of *stealing his own car*. Of course, stories about the shootings abound, and in Oakland, more than 100 protesters were arrested as they took to the streets to demand justice for Grant. Organizations like the Color of Change are speaking up on behalf of the victims, and demanding we do the same, while radio personalities like Warren Ballentine are using their syndicated radio shows to keep the stories fresh on the minds of black folks.

Still, after the roar dies down, after the police officers get off (they almost always do), after we commit the victims' names to the long list of young black men who've died or been abused at the opposite end of a police officer's gun/nightstick/bathroom plunger (Sean Bell. Amadou Diallo. Abner Louima. Patrick Dorismond. Michael Carpenter. I could go on and on and on), who will stop the same from happening to my stepson?

How do I protect my normal, brilliant, college-bound, sweet, black boy?

The urge to protect him will never leave me, this is the unfortunate rite of passage for every parent of a black boy. Once they are big enough and old enough to move out into the world without us holding their hands or watching over them, they are going to be vulnerable to the biases and misperceptions and stereotypes and downright hatred of an overwhelming number of cops, transit officers, sheriff's deputies, and other law enforcement officials who will cross our children's paths over the next 40–50 years of their lives. I suppose the best we can do is hope that one day Mazi will put in enough years so that he can have the same worry about his own child as we have for him.

And agitate.

And pray. —*JANUARY 2009*

CHAPTER 51

Racist Selfie Mocking Black Child Makes Me Remember Why I Never Hired White Sitters

I N THE LATEST EDITION of "Saying Stupid Shit on Facebook Will Get You Dragged by Black Twitter, Fired from Your Job and Lead to a Life Of Ruin," a white guy who posted a picture of his coworker's three-year-old black son, inspiring a thread of racist slavery jokes about the toddler, is now out of a job and trying to salvage his edges from a vicious Internet snatching.

To be clear, Gerod Roth, who went by the name Garis Hilton on Facebook, deserved what he had coming. Without the knowledge or consent of Sydney Shelton, his Polaris Marketing Group coworker, Roth posted that picture of Shelton's son, Cayden Jace, and, for two weeks, left it there with a grip of foul jokes up and down the thread, including "Help feed this poor child today," "I didn't know you were a slave owner," "Kunta . . . kunta kinte," "But Massuh, I dindu nuttin," and even a cover of a Little Black Sambo book. Roth later chimed in, calling the toddler "feral." As in a wild animal.

Sheldon didn't find out about the exploitation of her son until concerned Facebook users shared the image and thread with the hopes of finding Cayden's parents. According to Colorlines, two weeks had passed by before the mother realized her child was being exploited on the Internet by her fellow employee, who had nary a problem working every day with Sheldon and kee-keeing with her son, even as he and his friends made fun of the toddler online.

That is some nasty, shady, disgustingly foul mess right there—enough, I know, to have made even the most sane, rational black mama want to wait for him out in the parking lot with a posse and maybe a choice bat or two. Luckily for Roth, Cayden's mother has sense. She reserved her anger and instead focused on changing the narrative blazing across search engines—a narrative that describes her son as everything but what he is: a beautiful, smart, sweet, funny black boy who deserves the respect and protection we afford to children.

"I just want people to understand that Cayden is the absolute opposite of what they said of that picture," she told Colorlines. "He's the smartest kid. He's got such a big personality."

With the help of an online friend and advocate, she also started the hashtag #HisNameIsCayden so that rather than training attention on Roth, she could shine a light on her heart and joy. The hashtag was accompanied by a passionate Facebook post and a grip of gorgeous pics of her and her son.

Sheldon's job also threw its support behind the mother and her son by firing the hell out of Roth, and releasing a passionate Twitter statement of its own, praising Sheldon and her baby. Michael De Grassa Pinto, the company's president, wrote:

> This morning I was disgusted to learn that one of my former employees made several racially charged comments on his personal Facebook page. Even worse, the comments were directed toward the son of another employee. It breaks my heart that Sydney and her adorable son Cayden were subjected to such hateful, ignorant and despicable behavior. Cayden visits my office almost every afternoon after daycare, he's sat at my dinner table and I consider him a part of the PMG family. The atrocious lies, slander and racism he

and his mother have been forced to endure are wholly intolerable. Myself and the entire PMG family in no way condone this kind of behavior and would never willingly associate with anyone who does. It has no place in this world. PMG has terminated the employee responsible and will ensure that none of the business that we associate with will ever do business with him again.

I couldn't be more proud of the way Cayden's mom handled the situation, or her company for having her back and saying that under no scenario is what Roth did unacceptable. But I promise you, the story dug up all kinds of reservations I had when the girlpies were little and I was all new and leery about leaving them in the care of others and I was on what seemed like an endless search for a sitter. The truth is, I didn't trust the idea of having a white nanny watching my black daughters. I just couldn't. I couldn't bring myself to trust that a white woman (or man) could and would know how to do the basics, like lotion their skin after a bath every time, or style their kinky hair without breaking it or having them leave the house looking like they were wearing a bird's nest on the top of their heads, or know how to talk to them about the beauty of a Donny Hathaway song or a Stevie Wonder lyric or the chocolate in a juicy Kadir Nelson illustration.

Mostly, though, I was scared to death that a white nanny would do exactly what Roth did behind Sheldon's back: mock and encourage racist behavior directed at my children, or, worse, slay my children's self-esteem with sideways comments about things they can't change and that I've vowed to spend their lifetimes teaching them how to love: their skin, their hair, their black bodies, their culture, their family, their souls. It was just best for everyone involved that I hire a sitter who could, shall I say, hit the ground running with knowing how to handle the racial aspects of caring for black children, and stick to letting my children around white adults I liked, trusted, vetted, and spent an incredible amount of time around to be sure we wouldn't have the equivalent of a racist-selfie-mocking-black-child moment.

Yes, I know this sounds unfair. Some may even consider me intolerant. But I'm human and black and wise enough to know the limitations of others and especially my own: had Roth or someone like him done that to one of my babies, you would not be writing nice things about me. You'd be raising my bail. —*OCTOBER 2015*

CHAPTER 52

Black Children and "White People Sports"

LOOK HERE: I've been doing TV commentary as a journalist—gabbing about everything from politics and entertainment to race and parenting—since the mid '90s, and I've sparred with the best over some controversial topics: Jack Kevorkian, Trayvon Martin, whether black parents who hit their kids with switches are practicing plantation discipline, the best ways to talk to children about sex. In an appearance on the *Meredith Vieira Show*, I added another doozie to the list: black children and white people sports.

Oh, yeah, you read that correctly. There I was on Meredith's mom panel, debating about whether it's safe for kids to play football, when fellow panelist, New York radio deejay Carolina Bermudez, announced that she wants her "half-Latino, half-white" son (her description, not mine) to play "white sports."

White sports, yo.

Carolina's remark, all weird and inappropriate and a smidge snooty and a lot ignorant, even made fellow panelist Mel B., a.k.a. Scary Spice, truly one of the most nonracial black women on the planet, uncomfortable. And best believe, it encouraged an *epic* side-eye from yours truly. Meredith, who, after playing the amiable referee for years on *The View* may sense a verbal smackdown when she sees one, managed to steer the convo away from the foolery before I could get my boxing gloves on, but trust me, had we had the time, had we had the space, had my garden of f*cks been barren, Carolina's ignorant statement would have been taken down.

I mean, consider the implications of what she's saying here: she wants her "half-white" son to tap into his good white folk side and play games that, what . . . are steeped in white privilege? That embrace a tradition of using economics and straight-up racism to bar black athletes from playing them? That open the door to "white gentlemen" rather than those big, black bucks that use their brute strength, muscle, and size to smash up people like animals?

When pressed, she tried to clean up her words by insisting that she simply wanted her son to play a game "where he can make a difference and he's not in danger," but really, the damage was done. Coloring noncontact sports, literally, in whiteness in this particular conversation about the dangers of football (a sport dominated by black men) opened the floodgates to a historic conversation steeped in cruel stereotypes and racist tropes about "other" black bodies.

Black athletes/men are dangerous.

Black athletes/men are violent.

Black athletes/men are barbaric.

Black athletes/men are prone to hurting good white folk.

White folk are safe . . . genteel . . . cunning . . . nonviolent . . . intelligent. More physically, mentally, socially, and emotionally fit for sports like tennis and golf and crew and, like, ultimate frisbee.

Of course, Caroline didn't say all this. But really, surely, she's a smart enough woman to know that when you unpack a conversation around "white sports" and black athletes, you unpack centuries of racist labels/jokes/beliefs that continue to rear their ugly heads. Like when world-champion tennis player Serena Williams, with her curvy, muscular, perfect-in-every-way chocolate body, slays on the tennis court but still gets called "manly" and "masculine" and "nigger" by the fans, and dogged by the game announcers, even when she's winning. Like when Tiger Woods won golf's Masters Tournament and his opponents "jokingly" asked if he'd be serving fried chicken at his championship dinner. Like when spectators waved bananas and tossed chicken wings on the ice when Joel Ward dared play ice hockey with the Washington Capitals.

If we must talk about the color divide in sports, then, well, let's go there. Let's talk about the exclusion of blacks—and hell, Latinos and Asians and every other person of color, for that matter—from the golf greens, tennis courts, swimming pools, rowboats, ski slopes and ice rinks. Let's talk about why it's so cost-prohibitive for mere average people to participate in these sports in meaningful ways. Let's talk about the racism people of color face when they do try to play. And yeah, let's talk about how black folks tend to dominate those sports if they do manage to slip in.

Simply put: the ugliness is real, still. The history sears, still. And Carolina's proclamation about "white sports" in the context of our conversation felt . . . gross. Even more so when, yesterday, she took to Twitter to dismiss her comments as a "joke" that her critics need to "get over."

Ha ha hell. No one's laughing, Carolina.

As the mother of athletes who have played on organized football, soccer, softball, basketball, tennis, track, and swim teams, I'd like to point out that athletes are just that—athletes. They play with heart and passion and prowess and intelligence, and their ability to excel in one sport translates rather easily to others because they're . . . well . . . athletes. Strip away the barriers and all that backwards-ass thinking about color dictating who should play what, and it really is that simple.

How about we stop harping on color and what "white sports" are and just let the kids play? —*FEBRUARY 2015*

CHAPTER 53

Racist College Culture & Black Student Survival at University

I DON'T KNOW WHY FOLKS are acting all shocked by this SAE video madness, as if despicably racist, "nigger"-filled rants by groups of white college boys are somehow new, fresh, unexpected, and unique. Any human who's ever stepped foot on the campus of a predominately white college or university can tell you with relative ease that this kind of behavior, that kind of brazen foolishness, those kind of animals, are all par for the course on the soils of American institutions of higher learning.

It's the same ol' story: members of the University of Oklahoma's chapter of Sigma Alpha Epsilon, a fraternity founded before the Civil War in the antebellum South, got busted singing a racist song about never letting black people pledge. Though the SAE video doesn't show the segregationist ditty in its entirety, the refrain repeated over and over again to the melody of "If You're Happy and You Know It"—"there will never be a nigger in SAE"— is interspersed with a reminder of the frat members' willingness to do what the good ol' boys of the Jim Crow South used to do to terrorize black folk into following their racist rules: "You can hang 'em from a tree, but he'll never sign with me." Of course, the entire bus is practically rocking as its passengers, clad in tuxedos, heading to an event at an exclusive golf club, sing the song with great gusto and glee. A separate Vine video shows the frat's house mother, looking like a Paula Deen understudy, repeatedly and rapidly saying the word "nigger" while she giggles into the camera—like she's *really* used to letting it just roll off her tongue.

In typical fashion, the fraternity's national chapter issued an apology and put an ocean's worth of distance between itself and its errant members, claiming in a statement that the song is not one it teaches SAE brothers and that it's totes cool with the University of Oklahoma's move to drop kick the local chapter off its campus. The statement went on to say that they're suspending the OU students from their fraternity, they're working with African Americans to "build a partnership that will address the need for additional training, awareness, and resources on cultural and diversity issues" and blah, blah, blah, blah, blah . . .

And right there is where it gets especially stupid. Because everyone pondering this thing—from the university to the fraternity to the members to the media and beyond—is acting like this is some isolated incident that goes away with a statement and an expulsion and a meeting with the Black Student Union.

It doesn't.

Racism on American campuses is as ingrained and regular and damn-near noneventful as rain is wet, grass is green, and sugar is sweet. Because, duh, the campuses are filled with Americans—all-too-many white folk who were raised at the knee of parents and grandparents and aunties and uncles and cousins and friends who can't stand blacks (Latinos, Asians, Middle Easterners, and Indians, and everyone else of color, too) and hold tight to stereotypes and privilege that makes them certain white folks are the shit and everyone else is nothing more than the soiled toilet tissue on the bottom of their shoes. This is not a white frat thing. This is not a southern university thing. This is not an isolated incident. This is America. This is fact.

I learned that much not more than half an hour into my college experience at my alma mater, Hofstra University, on Long Island, New York. My parents couldn't have been out of the parking lot after our teary goodbyes before one of my two roommates, a girl from the butt-crack of Pennsylvania, informed me that she'd never seen "a black girl in real life before." This while the other roommate, from Chicago, ran her fingers across my toiletries and, settling on my jar of DAX hair grease, asked me what it was for before informing me that while she'd seen black people before, she didn't know any personally.

I wasn't sure what to make of what they'd said, but I didn't know anyone on campus yet, so, operating on the "you all I got" philosophy, I pushed their treating me like a Martian aside and agreed to go with Chicago to meet some of her friends in a neighboring dorm. Hey, I had to start somewhere, right? Well, that was a disaster. While I stood in a corner of her friend's room, trying to figure out what I could say to fit in with these girls—all white—another girl came barging into the room, pissed. "That stupid nigger downstairs wouldn't let me into the door because I don't have my ID yet," she seethed, completely unaware that I was there until her friends, frozen and wide-eyed, introduced her to me, the black girl.

"I didn't mean nigger in a bad way," she insisted. "I meant nigger like, ignorant person. Not black."

I wish I could tell you that I had a pithy comeback, or that I punched her in the face in solidarity with my people or that I called her on her racist crap. But honestly, she caught me off guard, y'all. I did not expect to hear the word a half an hour into my time out in the "real world." I did not expect to have to confront the person who said it. I did not expect to be paired with roommates who'd never seen or talked to black people before and had only stereotypes and yes, racist beliefs, to work with before they met special, naive, nervous, "can't we all just get along" ol' me.

The experience grew me up real quick, trust. And by the time I left Hofstra, I was real clear on the ways of racist white folk.

But when I went to that school, I wasn't ready because no one prepared me for it. I'm the first and only one in my immediate family to go to and graduate from college and so it makes sense that my parents wouldn't know thing one about campus dynamics. But I'll be damned if I let my girlpies tap one of their manicured toes on the campus greens without understanding that American colleges and universities are but a mere microcosm of America, with a faction of racists who are often too young, stupid, and drunk to hide their sick, twisted thinking when it comes to race. They sit in classes as kind as you please during the daytime, but in the cover of night, they whoop and holler and piss all in the hallways and tear up furniture and fixtures and sexually assault young women and yell racist shit at black folk with impunity, knowing nothing will happen to them because the campus system, like the American system, is set up to protect them. To let them act any ol' kind of way because they're white and they just can. Campus security is too busy policing black students, professors, administrators, and workers to care that the others are tearing the campus apart and attacking and abusing students of color.

What those boys were doing in the SAE video was not new. It happens every second of the day in the dorm rooms, in the locker rooms, in the bleachers of the sporting events, and yes, at alcohol-fueled frat parties of every non-HBCU in the country. Don't believe me? Consider all the racist blackface, anti-black and -immigrant keggers these idiots host then splash on Instagram and Twitter, with an attitude that's totally, "Like, what? We're just having fuuuuun!"

While the University of Oklahoma's president should be applauded for his swift action to denounce the offending students, kick them out of school, ban the frat, and shutter SAE's campus house—real talk, those were boss moves—each of us has to stop acting as if this kind of behavior is rare and happens in a vacuum.

Racism on college campuses is systemic.

It is real.

It is pervasive.

Let's start the conversation there.

And rather than call in the good BSU folk to help white students understand why it's hurtful to sing "nigger" songs, how about we put that effort into giving black students the tools and mettle they need to make it through the race gauntlet they'll surely face on America's college campuses. Indeed, in America, period.

—MARCH 2015

THE MARTYRS

On Black Children, Race, and Lives That Mattered

The George Zimmerman Verdict Is Deeply Inhumane. This Is Why We Need to Keep Fighting.

W HO PRAYS FOR OUR SONS? When their bodies are bloodied, broken, and frozen in the footnotes of this, our complicated history, who falls to their knees, head bowed, hands outstretched through storm and cloud and toward the warmth of the sun, and prays for the boys, the fathers, the uncles and nephews and friends? Our brothers?

Whose tongue will confess when another Tracy Martin and Sybrina Fulton and another Ron Davis and Lucia McBath and another Dominika Stanley and Charles Jones and another Carol Gray and another Wanda Johnson and another Saikou and Kadiatou Diallo and another William and Valerie Bell and another Moses J. Stewart and Diane Hawkins and another Mamie Till have their hearts torn from their bodies with the news that Trayvon and Jordan and Aiyana and Kimani and Oscar and Amadou and Sean and Yusef and Emmett won't ever again make them laugh or hold their hands—won't ever bow their heads in church pews or rip open Christmas presents or inhale deep and blow out the birthday candles or say, simply, "I love you, Mommy," and "I love you, Daddy"? Who wipes their tears—our tears—when they and we know, too, that their babies—our babies—will never, ever come home?

This wicked system of things—it simply is not natural. The murders. The outcry. The half-assed investigations that seek placation, rather than justice. The, "No really, we give a fuck, but not really" stories flooding the eleven o'clock news that go ignored by the "real" Americans while they eat their microwave popcorn and keep up with the Kardashians and the Real Housewives of Wherever, unmoved save for their keyboard gangsta conservative (and always anonymous) racist rants in the HuffPo comments section.

You know what else is not natural? The getting away with it. *The. Getting. Away. With. It.*

Of course, there is no surprise in that part of it—the part where Zimmerman and the many like him who came before him walks free. Extreme sadness, yes. Anger, too. And disgust. Definitely disgust. But surprise? No. This is the American way. For us, there is no justice.

Just . . . us.

Still, it is becoming increasingly hard as an African American mother to explain and to instruct—to dream a world in which my babies can do/say/be as they please in the land of the free, where, clearly, they are not . . . free. When black children's bodies are stereotyped and policed and dissected and disregarded and taken without recourse, when something as simple as buying Skittles and wearing a hoodie in the rain can get you murked, when American law licenses white men to stalk, attack, shoot, and kill someone's baby and brag and giggle about it in front of an international audience, it's kind of hard to assure my kids that it's all going to be all right. Especially when I'm not convinced of this. How do we make our kids feel safe when *we* don't feel safe?

And so we are left with our fears. Fears that leaped out in Technicolor when the jury in the George Zimmerman murder trial pronounced him not guilty in the shooting death of Trayvon Martin. Our children are in the crosshairs. And Zimmerman's attorneys just laid out for the world to see a blueprint for how to buck down black boys and men and get away with it. The heart is heavy. And it throbs and aches.

This is normal. And it is okay. I cosign a Facebook status my writer friend, the brilliant and prolific dream hampton, sent up my timeline this past weekend: "Be in your pain. You are human and this verdict is deeply inhumane."

Inhumane.

Say that shit with your chest. From your gut. Because it is true and right and tamps down the hurt—just a little bit.

But even as we work through the pain, we must respond to it. James Baldwin once wrote in a 1970 letter to Angela Davis, then a political prisoner, that it was the duty of blacks to fight for her life as if it were our own, "For if they take you in the morning, they will be coming for us that night." I channel this thought as I talk to my own girls and my stepson about Trayvon and Zimmerman and the justice system and just us. I channel, too, Martin and especially Malcolm: "We declare our right on this earth . . . to be a human being, to be respected as a human being, to be given the rights of a human being in this society, on this earth, in this day, which we intend to bring into existence *by any means necessary.*"

I kick off my response by exercising the most human of responses—the most human of actions: I hug my babies and rub their backs and kiss their cheeks and let them know, for sure, that they are loved with abandon. That they are valued. And valuable. More precious than anything I claim. Even my breath. The very beat, even, of my heart.

And then we talk. And talk some more. About Trayvon. About Zimmerman. About the law. And the history of the American justice system and our place in that. And Emmett. And the Four Little Girls. And all the white men who walked free and clear as black mothers and fathers cried out over the caskets of their babies.

They must learn.

As *we* pray and confess, our children . . . must . . . learn.

And then, together, we fight.

With the might of the angels, with our babies on our backs, we fight. —*JULY 2013*

CHAPTER 55

ENOUGH.
(Don't Let Aiyana Jones Die in Vain.)

ER NAME WAS AIYANA JONES and she was only seven
years old. In the photo widely circulated after her death,
the dimples in her chocolate cheeks and that hand on her hip tell
a story. Maybe she was a little joker, all giggles and big on fun—
inquisitive, energetic, and a bit of a smarty-pants, with a tip of
nutty thrown in for good measure. I can almost see those fancy
twists flying in the wind—hear her colorful barrettes clacking
and dancing to the rhythm of her little girl dance. She reminds
me of my Lila, who, also age seven, is all of these things and
then some.

Aiyana could have easily been my child.

This matters to me because Aiyana is dead.

She was felled by a police officer's bullet during the execution
of a no-knock warrant at her grandmother's home. The police, acting on a tip that a homicide suspect was staying there, ran in to the
house, flash grenades and guns ablaze, with all of the bully tactics
of a stealth marine troop storming a terrorist hideout in Fallujah.
By the time the smoke and gunshots and chaos cleared, Aiyana lay
on the couch where she had been peacefully sleeping under her
favorite Disney blanket, bleeding to death from a gunshot wound
to the neck—yet another senseless casualty of police aggression in
urban (read: black) communities. Her daddy, forced to the ground
by the cops and denied the request to see about his daughter, lay

in his little girl's blood as he watched the light slowly, surely, fade from her eyes.

Aiyana joins a long line of black folk whose lives were cut short by aggressive police tactics that, pumped with adrenaline, heightened fear, and a laundry list of double standards reserved for communities of color, make for the lethal hail of bullets that claimed the lives of black folk across the land—Amadou Diallo, Patrick Dorismond, Sean Bell, Timothy Stansbury, Eleanor Bumpurs, Kathryn Johnston, the list goes on. When it comes to people of color and their communities, it never, ever seems to matter that this is a country that stakes its claim on the basic judicial tenet that citizens are innocent until proven guilty. It seems always to be shoot to kill now, sort it out later.

This philosophy never seems to apply in communities like Buckhead and Beverly Hills and Scarsdale and Grosse Pointe, where, I assure you, police brass are not authorizing and encouraging their officers to use military tactics to apprehend suspects, thus putting entire communities—including seven-year-old babies—in extreme danger.

When will this madness stop? How many more times must innocent people die before someone decides that it is simply unacceptable to continue to give police departments carte blanche to run roughshod through black and brown communities, patting down and gunning down as many people as they see fit—no matter their involvement, no matter the danger, no matter the cost—in the name of "justice" and "law and order"?

Of course, the police officer who shot Aiyana would have rathered his bullet didn't end that baby's life (though he and his fellow officers do get a serious side-eye for storming Aiyana's grandmother's house with TV cameras in tow, with the hopes that their dramatic apprehension of a murder suspect would make it onto the *Cops*-styled TV show, *48 Hours*. There have been claims, too, that before the officers stormed the house, they were told by neighbors that children were present, as evidenced by a cadre of toys strewn about the lawn). But the officer's intentions aren't the issue here. What does need to be questioned, challenged, and rallied against are the policies that allow police departments across the country—specifically in urban neighborhoods—to use military tactics against their own citizens, as if they are not a part of the fabric of this land—as if they are living in an occupied state where people in uniforms have the ultimate right to violate your home, run roughshod over your most precious possessions, and hurt fellow human beings, then hide behind reckless policies to justify such cruel, inhuman actions.

Stray dogs get rounded up with more humanity.

The bottom line is that kids don't pick their parents or their communities or their homes or the people who care for them. It is an accident of birth that put Aiyana in that Detroit neighborhood, and not in, say, the White House. And so it is incumbent upon the grown-ups—particularly the caretakers, and especially those who are charged with serving and protecting us—to, in all the things that we do, protect the babies first.

At all costs.

Because the baby on the couch might be the next Sasha Obama.

Or my Lila.

Or a child you know.

Maybe even your own.

Please, Lord, no more of this. Tonight, I say a prayer for Aiyana and her father and her grandmother and their family; pray that they'll find the strength to carry on after becoming the latest victims of the war being waged in black and brown communities the world over.

I pray, too, that Aiyana, the pretty little chocolate girl with the bouncing twists and the dimpled smile, did not die in vain.

—*MAY 2010*

CHAPTER 56

No Safe Place for Black Children

A 12-YEAR-OLD shot by police this weekend is dead. The CHILD, Tamir Rice, was playing with his sister and a friend in a Cleveland, Ohio, PARK when a grown ass drunk in a bar across the street dialed up police and said a man was waving around a gun, "scaring the shit out of everyone." That drunk went on to tell the dispatcher that the PERSON they were all scared of was "probably a JUVENILE" and that the gun was "probably fake," but neither the caller, dispatcher, nor cops could be bothered by those details. The police officers responding to the call showed up, guns drawn, told a 12-YEAR OLD CHILD to put his hands in the air and then executed the BOY when he reached for his TOY.

Tamir Rice, a 12-year-old shot by police, is dead.

Don't say s— to me about how real his TOY gun looked. Don't say s— to me about legit fears people may have had about the TOY gun or the CHILD who was PLAYING with it in the PARK—in an open-carry state that allows its (white) citizens to wield weapons in public with impunity as part of the law the citizens themselves approved. Don't say s— to me about concerned citizens and cops doing their jobs. Don't say s— to me about how a 12-YEAR-OLD BOY PLAYING in a PARK with his friends, completely unaware of drunk neighbors fearing CHILDREN, should have responded to cops screaming at him to raise his hands. Don't say s— to me about mistakes.

Tamir Rice, a 12-year-old shot by police, is dead.

Instead, let's talk about these key words: 12-YEAR-OLD CHILD. PERSON. JUVENILE. BOY. TOY. PLAYING. PARK. Tamir Rice was a 12-YEAR-OLD CHILD. A PERSON. A JUVENILE. A BOY who was PLAYING with a TOY in the PARK. You know what else he was? A BLACK BOY.

But in America, there is not room for black boys and girls to be children. Ever. Consider these words from child advocate Dr. Stacey Patton, who delivered this powerful speech, "There's No Such Thing As Black Childhood: How the Murders of Trayvon Martin & Mike Brown Are Rooted In Jim Crow Racial Ideology," at the University of Kentucky College of Law:

> From Emmett Till and Mike Brown to legions of other young people whose names and lives have been violently lost to the hidden holocaust of racial history in America, white supremacy REQUIRES the intentional, insidious, and pervasive devaluation and destruction of black childhood.
>
> Rather than a sanctuary from harm, or an eventual route to full adult citizenship, white supremacy REQUIRES that childhood for black Americans be imagined as devoid of innocence and marked by various processes of imposing stigma, oppression, and danger.
>
> White supremacy REQUIRES that black childhood not be defined, in the Western sense, as a distinct period grounded in a linear set of unfolding stages toward maturation, civility, responsibility, and citizenship worthiness, but that it be imagined as undifferentiated from black adulthood and that it be accelerated toward intellectual, spiritual, social, sexual, and physical death.
>
> And, white supremacy REQUIRES the

participation of black people (sometimes unintentionally) in that dehumanization process—a process which unfolds at each developmental milestone in the life of the child—embryonic development, the moment of birth, infancy, adolescence, and puberty. Each life stage is seized by various actors, racialized, and baked into popular images, attitudes, behaviors, educational and medical practice, policing, and social policies around child welfare and juvenile justice. One way we see the evidence is through the repeated failure to prosecute white men who murder unarmed black children . . .

Friends, racism prevents us from collectively fixing our lips to say, "a child was killed" when the victims are black. In America, the notion of what is a child and who gains access to the category, affords levels of protection, sympathy, innocence, remorse, redemption, and the privilege to be a kid, and even making mistakes without the consequences of a social or physical death.

With Dr. Patton's words ringing in my ears and my heart, I say again, a 12-year-old shot by police this weekend is dead. Tamir Rice was A CHILD. PLAYING WITH A TOY IN THE PARK WITH HIS FRIENDS.

The drunk did not have to call the cops.

The cops should not have shot this child.

Tamir's mother should not be mourning her son.

Still, here we are again, we black parents screaming from the rooftops and in cap locks that OUR CHILDREN MATTER—that, in the name of TRAYVON and JORDAN and AIYANA and MIKE and all the other black children who've been bucked down by

people with callous regard for our babies' humanity, this . . . must
. . . STOP. Another black child is dead. Another set of black parents is grieving. Another community has been torn apart. And our hearts, battered and bruised and worn from the continual shock and anger, are shattered and stomped into the ground like dust, left to blow in a bitter wind. Like we're nothing.

When it happens, and the police shrug their shoulders and get to denying, and the authorities in charge start rolling their tanks and armed troops through American neighborhoods and the national news treats the death of yet another BLACK CHILD like it's normal to buck down kids in American streets, don't take to the mic and ask black parents to be calm.

Fuck calm.

This . . . madness . . . must . . . STOP.

By Any Means Necessary. —NOVEMBER 2014

Five Valuable Lessons for What Kids Should Do in Volatile Encounters with Strangers and Cops

I DON'T KNOW a single black parent with eyes, a heart, and blood pumping through their veins who can watch the video of the Texas cop attacking black children at a pool party without making the screw face and declaring some version of the following: "Had that been my kid, y'all would be digging in your mattresses for my bail money or I'd be up under the damn jail or dead." What other kind of reaction could one possibly have after witnessing the one officer running amok, performing a wild-eyed *Paul Blart: Mall Cop*-meets-Jean-Claude-Van-Damme parody while tossing bathing-suit-clad black boys to the ground, pointing his gun at a group of unarmed kids and driving his fat knees and sweaty crotch into the back of a bikini-clad ninth-grade girl? Like, seriously, who *does* this to children? And how can anyone look at what is happening in that video, or read any of the myriad stories detailing what happened, and not cry out/get pissed/want to put the paws on this fool?

What happened at that McKinney, Texas, community pool is nothing less than disgusting—yet another highly charged, high-stakes incident in a long line of excessive force used against black children simply trying to . . . be. Consistently, our babies' very humanity is questioned, criticized, policed, and met with radically excessive response, particularly when they are being their most purely joyful kid selves: on the way back from buying Skittles, playing "cops and robbers" with a toy gun, building forts, listening to their favorite music; and, in the case of the Craig Ranch North community pool in McKinney, going for a cool swim with friends on the last day of school. In her TheRoot.com essay, "McKinney, Texas: Rage Is Our Rightful Response to Anti-Black Racism," Kirsten West Savali makes a keen, clear-eyed observation:

> This white supremacist infrastructure is constructed to keep our children gridlocked while their white counterparts cruise on by in the high-occupancy vehicle lane. And at each checkpoint, there are monsters in uniform who will desecrate their black flesh and tap dance on their bones without giving it a minute's thought.

At the very least, in the case of the McKinney pool party, it was clear even to top police brass in the well-to-do Dallas suburb that at least one police officer, Corporal Eric Casebolt, overreacted—so much so that he was suspended pending an investigation. A statement by the American Civil Liberties Union of Texas makes plain why officers should be held accountable for the resulting mess: the police response "appears to be a textbook case of overuse of force," the statement reads. "A well-trained police department would have responded more cautiously, with less hostility and using sophisticated crowd-control methods that favor de-escalation not escalation. Without question, guns were not needed and in fact risked turning a group of partying teenagers into a violent encounter that could have turned deadly."

Say word.

But, as the mother of three, including two African American teenage girls, I'm concerned not just about what the police did wrong, but what I need to be saying to and teaching my daughters, who could just as easily find themselves in the middle of this kind of situation—this kind of madness.

Oh, be clear: that's not an overstatement. See, my family and I have lived an entire lifetime in predominately white spaces where our very presence, at the very least, has been repeatedly questioned and, in some instances, railed against. What do you know about cops stopping your son at the entrance of his own subdivision and being told, "you better not let me catch you in this neighborhood again," despite that his parents owned a home there?

What do you know about neighbors sending "community" emails warning everyone to keep an eye out for people who "don't belong" because they caught sight of some black boys walking home from school?

What do you know about white mothers pulling their kids away from children of color at the park under the assumption that their parents are gang members or that you're an interloper from the bad part of town using "their" slide, swings, and play areas because they're nicer than those in the 'hood they assume you're from?

What do you know about having "neighbors" call the property manager on your family because someone decided there were too many of "you" at the pool, despite that you're clearly having a birthday party, you secured and paid for a permit to do so, and all those splashing black kids weren't nearly as disruptive as the fresh-out-of-college (white) residents hosting a bong and beer-game party with a bunch of visitors just feet away?

Each of these things has, indeed, happened to me and my family, and only by the grace of sweet Baby Jesus, we got little more than our pride slapped and our feelings hurt. But had any of those incidents escalated into someone calling the police on my kids and the responding officers escalating the situation into something rivaling the McKinney incident, I'm not so sure my daughters would know how to conduct themselves and do what they could to stay out of the epicenter of the madness.

Here's what I and my husband, coauthor of *Justice While*

Black, an advice book for families on how to avoid and navigate the criminal justice system, will be talking to our daughters about after we show them the video of the Texas cop attacking black children who look like them:

1. If racist adults talk crazy to you, do not stick around to get into an argument with them. This is supposedly how the entire incident at the community pool started—with a white woman taunting the black pool guests by telling them they should "go back to Section 8 housing." When the kids told her she was being racist, the lady is said to have physically attacked the 19-year-old pool party host. What we're advising our girls to do: try to be calm, do not engage them, walk away from their crazy, and find an adult who can be a surrogate advocate. That last part is particularly important because if a white person calls the cops on you after an altercation, whether verbal or physical, you need to understand that the cops will most likely take the side of the adult. Specifically, the white adult. Do not stick around to continue to be insulted or to have them arrange for you to get in trouble for their racist behavior.

2. Practice streets smarts—even when you're in the suburbs. We want our girls to be completely aware of their surroundings, to know when it's time to leave, and how to behave if they can't get away. This means that if something is popping off, it's just not a good idea to stick around and watch what goes down—especially if cop cars are pulling up. Walk—don't run—away calmly and get a safe distance away from the drama. Once away, call your parents or an adult who can come get you. We will be arriving with our lawyer.

3. If you cannot calmly move away from the action or a police officer tells you to stop, stop and do what he says. This is especially important when an out-of-control cop is doing combat rolls on the grass, cursing and waving his gun around like he's an extra in a D-level, straight-to-video action flick. He is hyped and looking for a reason to hurt someone. Know that your first order of business is to try not to be the person he hurts. Do not give him a reason to set his sights on you: don't curse back (seriously, you are not on the set of *Love & Hip Hop Atlanta*—do not pop off at the mouth), don't ask questions, don't try to state the case for why he's wrong and you're right. Do exactly as he says. This does not make you a punk or weak or a discredit to your race. But it does increase your chances of staying alive.

4. Collect as much information as you can. Look for badge numbers, names, police car plates, and any other identifying characteristics of the police officers involved. If it is safe to do so, videotape what is happening around you. These are the kinds of details you'll need to have so that when we adults get involved, we have more of a chance to hold these men accountable for their actions.

5. If you are taken into police custody, do not say a word. Not. One. Word. Call your parents and make sure that they show up with a lawyer. This part is most important. Tell them to bring a lawyer. A cop's job is to put you into the system and you are not going to talk your way out of it, as if the police made a mistake. When you try, you're giving away your constitutional right to remain silent and can easily implicate yourself—even if you've done nothing wrong. Jails are filled with innocent people who thought they could apply reason and logic to get themselves out of trouble. The system is not set up to help you. Let a lawyer who is trained to deal with the system do her job—period.

Always, the goal for kids should be to return home safely to their parents. That's what we parents want. That should be what the kids want, too—to fight another day. Hell, to see one. It is important to me that my daughters understand that I am by no means blaming the black children of McKinney for the police brutality they faced that day at the pool; what the cops did was wrong. Period, full stop. But there are lessons to be learned there for our babies, too. It's our job to teach them. —*JUNE 2015*

CHAPTER 58

Seriously, Can We Stop Calling Cops on Little Black Kids Already?

WE HADN'T YET MOVED any furniture into our new place so there were lots of empty rooms and open spaces—perfect for cartwheels and handstands and robust games of tag. For kids, basically, to be kids. So I didn't give even a second's thought to my daughters and their cousins doing what they do as I inspected our apartment and started visualizing in my mind's eye how I'd arrange the furniture and where I'd hang my favorite artwork and how long it would take for me to be done with it all so I could have a few friends over for a housewarming with wine. Lots of wine.

And then came the knock. Not even 10 minutes after I'd pushed the key into the door. It was building security. A "neighbor" was complaining about the noise. Apparently, there was lots of banging. And loud laughing. And doors slamming. None of which I thought was especially loud or egregious, but somehow, it warranted a phone call to the authorities. As did, apparently, my "loud" music and all the "bumping noises" that were made as we moved our furniture into the apartment a couple weeks later. That complaint triggered an email from the community manager.

Welcome to the neighborhood.

I mean, I get that not everybody is into children or Jay-Z and Jill Scott pumping from Bose speakers at 9 p.m. on a Friday night, but really? Calling "the law" on the new neighbors rather than, oh, I don't know, knocking on the door, introducing yourself and letting me know that what we were doing could be heard in their small corner of our building would have been a much more neighborly way of handling the situation. And maybe even making a new friend who would be more inclined to respect reasonable boundaries rather than think of evil, awful ways to skirt right on the line of inappropriate just to annoy the crap out of The Evil Ones.

This is the way of The Evil Ones, you know—the people who take great pride in policing the homes/yards/space of others and then totally turn up when they see something/somebody that colors the stereotypes to which they cling. Think George Zimmerman stalking, attacking, and killing young black male Trayvon Martin. Think Michael Dunn hearing Hip Hop music blaring from a car full of black teens and pumping nine bullets into said vehicle, killing Jordan Davis for talking back. Think Rodney Bruce Black, the 62-year-old white man who shot and killed brothers Garrick Hopkins and Carl Hopkins, Jr., as they inspected their newly purchased home and property, which was adjacent to Black's yard.

Or consider what happened to sweet Omari Grant, an 11-year-old child from Henry County, Georgia, who allegedly had a cop point a gun at his face and then order him and his friends to lie facedown and spread eagle on the ground for . . .

wait for it . . .

wait for it . . .

Building a tree house in his backyard.

You read that right: little Omari, all of two years into double digits, says he and his friends were verbally and physically abused by a police officer after said cop was called to the yard by a neighbor policing the boys' movements. They were building a tree house with tree limbs and brush. The neighbor who called the cops on them thought something more nefarious was going on. In an interview with WSB-TV, Edgar Dillard, the neighbor's husband, said his wife called police on the little boys because they were breaking limbs off a tree. "There were falling hazards, tripping hazards, all types of hazards," Dillard said. "So no.1 was concern for the children and concern for the environment."

But we know what happens when black boys and nosy neighbors and cops with guns are involved: the potential for disaster and serious harm and injury to the boys is damn near inevitable. Poor little Omari told his mother he was scared for his life, and told WSB-TV he lay down on the ground and took the cop's abuse because, "I was thinking that I don't want to be shot today," he said, "so I just listened to what they said."

Let's be very clear about this thing: his fear is valid.

Of course, his mother filed a complaint against the cops for using excessive force against her son; police officials say they're looking into the incident to determine whether the cops were in the wrong; but in the meantime, police officers who pull guns out on little black boys for building tree houses in their backyards continue to carry firearms and wear badges and patrol neighborhoods in Henry County, waiting for nosy neighbors to call the cops on black kids for being . . . kids.

I suppose that talking to the boys herself would have proven too much for Mrs. Dillard. Walking over to Omari's house and introducing herself to his mom and letting her know she was concerned her little boy would get hurt would have proved equally hard, huh? Better to call the law and get all neighborhood watch à la George Zimmerman with it because who needs to treat black neighbors like . . . neighbors? Like they belong?

Lucky for my neighbors, I have a nice streak in me. And occasionally, with some pep talks from the hubs, it rears its head, as was the case after our neighbors sent building security to my door the second time in only one week of living at our place. I went to my local Kroger, bought a bunch of plants and knocked on the doors of the two neighbors who live on either side of us and the ones who live above and below us respectively. I introduced myself like a good neighbor, gave each of them my business card with my personal cell phone number scribbled on it, a plant, and explained that though I'd lived in apartments before, my daughters, who'd only lived in houses their whole lives, needed to get used to the idea of sharing their private space with others living all around them. But, I added, it would be great if everyone understood that really, they're little girls and they're full of life and they do kid stuff that sometimes is noisy. "Respect that, and I'll make sure they respect you," I promised.

That, after all, is the neighborly thing to do. —*APRIL 2014*

The Politics of Raising Black Children

CHAPTER 59

Newt Gingrich to Poor Black Mothers and Children: Pick Up a Broom, Lazy Asses.

S WEET BABY JESUS—serial sexual harasser and unapologetic adulterer Herman Cain finally crawls back into his hole and now we gotta watch serial cheater and crook Newt Gingrich take over the airwaves, screeching about how child labor laws, especially in the 'hood, are "truly stupid," nine-year-olds should be able to work as school janitors, and poor black mothers are a bunch of tragically lazy effers raising a bunch of even lazier effers?

I'm not making this up. Here's what this nutjob said: "Really poor children in really poor neighborhoods have no habits of working and have nobody around them who works. So they literally have no habit of showing up on Monday. They have no habit of staying all day. They have no habit of 'I do this and you give me cash' unless it's illegal."

insert image of Denene making dead fish eyes

This right here? *This mess right here?* It's more lethal than any instance of Herman Cain shoving his hands up a woman's skirt or breaking out into an a cappella version of "Amazing Grace" to explain why his 13-year jumpoff is making the TV rounds. Newt, the architect of the mean-spirited, early 1990s Contract with America, is waging war against our society's most vulnerable: the working poor, the unemployed, and their children, many of whom are African American and Latino.

So that we're all clear, Newt's talking out the side of his whole ass. In his *New York Times* column, "Newt's War on Poor Children," Charles M. Blow sets the facts straight: three out of four poor, working-aged adults have jobs—half of them full-time, a quarter of them part-time. He adds that census data shows that most poor children live in households with at least one working parent (hello—single moms!), and even a third of children living in extreme poverty—defined as a household living at least 50 percent below the poverty level—have one working parent. That translates into what you and I already know: that the problem isn't lazy parents—it's being stuck with jobs that pay no money while millionaires like Newt work tirelessly to dismantle every stitch of the little bit of support poor families need to simply survive. Dap and a bro shoulder bump to Charles for adding this:

> [Newt's] statement isn't only cruel and, broadly speaking, incorrect, it's mind-numbingly tone-deaf at a time when poverty is rising in this country. He comes across as a callous Dickensian character in his attitude toward America's most vulnerable— our poor children. This is the kind of statement that shines light on the soul of a man and shows how dark it is.

Don't get it twisted: Herman Cain was a UniverSoul Circus sideshow. There was no way in hell he was going to be the ringmaster. But Newt? Dude is being lifted by a bunch of ignorant, callous Americans salivating over his chance to decimate the very programs that help brown babies eat, brown mamas live, brown families get and stay healthy, and our community survive in the middle of the worst, most debilitating economic times of our generation.

Y'all better get like Dap in Spike Lee's *School Daze*.

Wake. Up. —*DECEMBER 2011*

CHAPTER 60

Dear Michele Bachmann: Shut Up about Black Moms and Breastfeeding

H ERE'S WHAT I'M GONNA NEED: I'm gonna need Michele Bachmann, Sarah Palin, Michelle Malkin, and Fox contributor Sandy Rios and them to sit down and hush. Like, now. Because their particular brand of ignorance is wearing on my one last good Mama Grizzly nerve.

Let me explain: as she celebrated the one-year anniversary of her Let's Move campaign, First Lady Michelle Obama said she now intends to train her anti-obesity efforts on early intervention, including making it easier for mothers to breastfeed—seeing as breastfed babies tend to be healthier and less likely to be obese as they grow. A centerpiece of the FLOTUS plan is to help put mothers on the good foot of breastfeeding from the moment they push out their babies—by working with hospitals to stop pushing formula and quit separating newborns from their moms, two practices that make it harder for mothers to start, practice, and sustain breastfeeding.

Mrs. Obama's plan would go hand-in-hand with new government measures designed to give breastfeeding moms support, including new IRS rules that make breastfeeding supplies deductible and reimbursable under flex spending plans, a new child nutrition law that provides more breastfeeding counseling and supplies to eligible low-income moms, and new federal rules that require some employers to give nursing moms break time and a dedicated place—other than the bathroom—to pump milk.

So let's see: hospitals will be asked to do right by new moms, low-income moms will be given the support they need to breast-feed if they choose to do so, and moms will catch a financial break from the most expensive part of breastfeeding their newborns.

And somehow, this is a *bad* thing in the eyes of the Tea Party princesses who strut around talking about how they're all about women and moms and family values and whatnot.

Now, I don't pretend to subscribe to anything Bachmann and her ilk have to say. Neither have I ever been compelled to speak up publicly about their particular brand of politics. So not worth my valuable brain matter. But Bachmann went on the attack after Mrs. Obama promised to do more to get black moms breastfeeding—bizarrely accusing FLOTUS of some kind of left-ist, anti-business conspiracy to form "a nanny state." Later, Rios was prancing all over Fox News, talking about how she's "in favor" of Mrs. Obama helping black women, but giving working mothers time and a place to nurse and pump their breast milk "is not right." Palin jumped on the bandwagon with some nonsense that was so confused and confusing, I absolutely refuse to spend my precious time trying to make hay of it.

Insert image of Denene giving all three of them a massive side-eye.

Really, y'all? *Really?!*

Am I the only one who sees the ridiculousness of these women and their asinine arguments? Because I absolutely cannot understand why women would be so willing to go hard against policies that actually *help* women do womanly things—like feed their babies in a clean environment without threat of losing their jobs. What's more? I don't appreciate nan one of them trying to frame this conversation on behalf of black mothers. Because I can guarantee you, they haven't the slightest clue the barriers black moms have to hurdle to get to what my friend Akiba Solomon called the "very natural, very basic way of nurturing our babies and ourselves."

I promise you, I damn near needed a cape, Wonder Woman's magical lasso, and a special order from the president and sweet Baby Jesus to get the support I needed as a black mom to breast-feed. Now mind you, when I had my babies, a lot of things went right for me: I had a supportive husband who did more than the average man when it came to diaper/feeding/burping/bathing duty; I had employers that let me pile up my vacation days for an extended maternity leave; and I had the cold hard cash I needed to make sure my babies had everything they needed to get the healthy start my ob-gyn, pediatrician, and every baby book on the planet said would be best.

Still, when I gave birth to my first baby in a hospital in Harlem, the nurses made quick work of handing me a "gift bag" with Similac, shoving a pacifier in my baby's mouth to quiet her, and disappearing for, literally, hours—leaving me to figure out on my own how to get my baby to latch on to my breast and nurse. By the time one arrived to my hospital room to "help me" feed my newborn—bottleful of formula in tow—I'd nearly allowed my baby to tear off my nipple from pulling her off my boob the wrong way. Five minutes with a lactation consultant, or hell, a nurse who believed I could, should, and would nurse, would have saved me hours of frustration and grief. Luckily, I was determined. And the nurse took pity on me and gave me a number for La Leche League so I could get some sound advice on how to feed my kid. But what about the black mom who didn't have access to the books or a dedicated doctor or a supportive network of friends to encourage her to breastfeed? Baby formula was likely going to be the food of choice for her newborn.

And don't even get me started on what it was like to be a working mom who pumped breast milk while on the job. Again, I was lucky: I was a journalist and had a pretty loose schedule that didn't keep me tied down to my desk, so disappearing for 15 minutes to pump really wasn't that big of a deal. But when I had my Mari, the only place to pump my milk was the bathroom. So I bought myself a car adaptor for my $200 pump and expressed in my car. Mind you, I had to walk past the dedicated room for smokers—we dubbed it The Butt Hutt—to get to my car. Imagine that? The bosses didn't have a problem finding a spare room and filling it with expensive, cozy furniture so that my coworkers—mostly men—could be as comfortable as could be while they shoved cancer sticks in their mouths, but no one could spare so much as a broom closet with a plastic chair so I could have some privacy and a funkless space to gather food for my baby.

Three years later, when I had my Lila and was working in a different, smaller office, I again faced pumping in the bathroom—a nasty little two-stall space where women peed and pooped and changed their tampons and farted and threw up and goodness knows what else. There was no way in hell I was going to gather my baby's food in there. So I regularly kicked my superiors out of their offices so that I could handle my business privately and in a reasonably clean environment.

But what about the breastfeeding mom who works on a factory line? Or at McDonald's? Or who doesn't have enough of a personal relationship with her bosses to get some alone time in his/her office to pump? Or who would love to breastfeed but can't so much as afford the pump that would allow her to collect her baby's food when she goes back to work, let alone the unpaid breaks and hostile attitudes she'd have to endure to conduct said collections?

I won't bother to get into the almost pathological resistance African American moms face from family and friends when it comes to breastfeeding. It. Is. No. Joke.

And so the last thing any of us need is for the likes of Bachmann, Rios, Palin, et al. to try to act like they understand and care about what black moms need to help them and their babies get a great start and thrive while, in the same breath, they work overtime to try to tear down policies—both proposed and passed—that would make it so that we—AND ALL MOMS—can stop having to scratch and buck and fight to do something so basic and natural as breastfeed.

Clearly, they don't give a damn about us. And I'll bet you my bottom dollar none of us stand at the ready to even pretend to believe like they do. Mostly, I wish the Tea Party princesses would just sit down and shut up about breastfeeding and childhood nutrition already. At the very least, they need to keep our names out of their mouths.

This isn't a game for black moms and black children.

Or about politics.

It's literally about life and death for our babies.

—*FEBRUARY 2011*

CHAPTER 61

Wisconsin Senator Thinks Single Parenthood Is Child Abuse—and Proposes Bill to Make It So

A WISCONSIN LEGISLATOR authored a controversial bill that would force the state's health department to claim in literature that children from single-parent homes are probably victims of child abuse. The bill, proposed by Senator Glenn Grothman, a Republican in Wisconsin's state senate, would force the state Child Abuse and Neglect Prevention Board to create campaigns that would "emphasize nonmarital parenthood as a contributing factor to child abuse and neglect." In a state where 32 percent of the populace is comprised of single parents. Grothman's bill reads, in part:

> Section 1. 48.982 (2) (g) 2. of the statutes is amended to read:
>
> 48.982 (2) (g) 2. Promote statewide educational and public awareness campaigns and materials for the purpose of developing public awareness of the problems of child abuse and neglect. In promoting those campaigns and materials, the board shall emphasize nonmarital parenthood as a contributing factor to child abuse and neglect.
>
> Section 2. 48.982 (2) (g) 4. of the statutes is amended to read:
>
> 48.982 (2) (g) 4. Disseminate information

about the problems of and methods of preventing child abuse and neglect to the public and to
organizations concerned with those problems. In
disseminating that information, the board shall
emphasize nonmarital parenthood as a contributing factor to child abuse and neglect.

crickets

When I come across silliness like this, I'm tempted to dismiss
it—as I would some pesky little boy insulting me in the hallway at
the middle school. Because surely, no sane, reasonable adult could
propose such nonsense and think they should be taken seriously.
It's not even really worth it here to go into all the many different
ways that this is ridiculous, except to say that a good 70 percent
of the African American community, more than half of all moms
under age 30, and a third of all moms, period, are, according to
this fool, verging on criminality because they have kids but no ring.

But then I think about it some more and I recognize that I
can't just dismiss this kind of madness. The more that it goes unchecked, the more the Rick Santorums and the Newt Gingriches
and the Wisconsin legislators of the world think that there's wide-
spread support in the public for insane ideas like this. It encourages them to keep at it—to get even more ridiculous in conjuring
up these culture wars, designed to keep us fighting amongst ourselves and distracting us from the real issues that affect us, like
the economy and unemployment, the banking industry and our
401ks and the housing market—the dismantling of benefits and
the unraveling of our country's safety net for those in need. While
we spend precious money, resources, and brain power shooting
down legislation that would allow the government to rape women
seeking abortions, we Americans are being financially, physically,
mentally, and emotionally robbed by a bunch of men giggling all
the way to the bank.

At this rate 100 arrogant bankers in New York have probably done more damage to American children of this generation than the whole lot of single moms put together, but I suspect that Mr. Wisconsin legislature is not trying to haul them off to the local jail.

Just a little food for thought today. Chew it, digest it, and keep it in mind the next time your local elections come around. Stay home and the idiot next door will become the idiot in your state legislature—the one who will try to legally proclaim you're a criminal because you had a baby but not a husband. Vote with *your brain*, and maybe we can keep these crazies out of office and get down to the real work of saving our country. —*MARCH 2012*

CHAPTER 62

Teen Girls Can Suck It

A ND HERE WE GO AGAIN with politicians getting all up into our ovaries. This time, the Obama administration made a surprising move to shut down the Food and Drug Administration's recommendation that the morning-after pill be made available over the counter without age restrictions—a decision that forces teens to get a doctor's prescription before they try to stop unwanted pregnancies.

Even though FDA Commissioner Margaret Hamburg said that scientific data shows "there is adequate and reasonable, well-supported and science-based evidence that Plan B One-Step is safe and effective and should be approved for nonprescription use for all females of child-bearing potential," US Department of Health and Human Services Secretary Kathleen Sebelius vetoed the decision, saying that adolescent girls may not be mature enough to understand how to use the morning-after pill, which, when taken within 72 hours of having unprotected sex, is almost 90 percent effective at preventing pregnancy.

So, just so we're clear: a 15-year-old who had unprotected sex and knows that she doesn't want to be a mom is too immature to follow the directions on the box, but mature enough to birth and raise a baby?

Long. Blank. Stare.

So it's crystal: I'm anti-teen sex. The last thing I'm advocating is that we send out personal invitations to kids to have sex—protected or otherwise—and let them handle the consequences and repercussions of those specific actions—STDs, unwanted pregnancy, abortion—on their own. In my fantasy world full of perfection, unicorns, mermaids, and unlimited supplies of half-naked Idris Elbas slathered in chocolate-flavored glitter, human beings do not have sex until they've stood in front of God, the preacher, and their mama and daddy andnem and said, "I do, forever and ever Amen."

Alas, I live on this here planet. Where teenagers are getting it in. Whether we parents approve or not. Whether they can get down to the CVS to get condoms or not. Whether the clinic gives them birth control pills or not. Whether they have access to and the money for reproductive health and abortion services or not. Whether they have the superhuman ability and cold, hard cash to take care of a baby or not.

So my God, why do we keep throwing up roadblocks to services and medication that help female humans of childbearing age protect their bodies and plan when they want to become parents?

I'm sure the Obama administration has its reasons for blocking a science-based decision made by the very department charged with making them. I'd begin with the idea that the last thing the president wants to do is give conservatives the ammunition they need to launch an all-out anti-abortion assault on the upcoming 2012 presidential elections—a raucous debate sure to distract from the most pressing issues at hand: the crappy economy, soaring unemployment rates, Wall Street crooks and cronies, and Newt Gingrich's assault on the poor.

I just hate that by taking away teen girls' ability to get the morning-after pill when they need it—without a costly, hard-to-secure appointment at the doctor to get it in time enough for it to actually be effective—teen girls have become political roadkill. Yet again.

—DECEMBER 2011

CHAPTER 63

Marissa Mayer, Yahoo's New (Pregnant) CEO, Isn't Special

W HAT I REALLY WANT TO SAY is that Marissa Mayer, the new CEO of Yahoo who announced shortly after her landmark appointment this week that she's pregnant and due to give birth to a baby boy in October, is my hero. She is, after all, taking a sledgehammer to the glass ceiling—grabbing the corner office of a Fortune 500 company with a baby in her belly *and* vowing to take only a short working maternity leave with her firstborn so that she can get down to the business of ruling the world. Clearly, Mayer is convinced she can have it all, and to prove it, she's going for it, critics be damned.

Still, the raging debate about whether Mayer can balance her new gig with being a new mom, and whether Yahoo's decision to hire her despite her pregnancy signals a sea change in the way pregnancy is handled in the workplace, leaves me queasy and a tad ticked off that some very real issues are totally being missed here. Let's be clear: Mayer is a *boss*. She will slip into her new role at Yahoo and then she will go away and birth her baby in October and she will have her son on her breast and a husband by her side and a cell phone at each ear and enough money, flexibility, and staff at her beck and call to miss not one beat as the head of her company. It won't be easy, mind you—any woman who's pushed a baby from her loins, woken up at 1:27 a.m., 3:01 a.m. and 4:15 a.m. for diaper changes and feedings, and felt post-pregnancy hormones take over her body like the demons in *The Exorcist* can attest to this. But Mayer's got the resources to make it work. And, most importantly, the ability to make a *choice* to do so.

The debate, then, isn't really whether she can or should do it. The very real question is why do we still live in a presumably civilized society—one that stands so morally and righteously on a platform of "family values"—where a majority of mothers are still being denied the choice Mayer enjoys? What she's doing isn't new or revolutionary: every day, mothers across America with limited resources, incomes, and physical, mental, and emotional support squat in the fields of this land, birth their babies and then head back to the assembly lines and the secretary desks and the fast food restaurants without benefit of choice—the choice to either spend precious time with their newborns, head back to work quickly because they *want* to do their jobs, or pull together a combination of the two so that they can be moms and good workers. America's ridiculously arcane maternity leave laws, which benefit only a sliver of our country's moms, make the balance impossible—especially for regular moms with regular jobs. Basically, most working moms.

So you'll have to excuse me if I'm not handing the "hero" cape to Marissa Mayer. It's much too tattered with the blood, sweat, tears, and breast milk of working mothers who are barely hanging on, who don't have choices, who lack the support system and the money and the status to enjoy their ideal mom experience—the one that works for babies and the women who birth them. How much you want to bet that the DNA of a Yahoo secretary or janitor or cafeteria worker is on that tattered cape? Marinate on that. Discuss. —*JULY 2012*

CHAPTER 64

The Fake Mommy Wars

I DISLIKE THEM down to their expensive dirty drawers but I give Mitt and Ann Romney and their Republican Party credit: they're masters at turning nonissues into politically expedient grenades—the kind that expertly explode any unified stance women, mothers, and the middle class might take. No such thing was more true than the ridiculously big deal the Romneys made out of Democratic talking head Hilary Rosen's assertion that Ann Romney, an uber rich stay-at-home mom of five who raised her kids on her husband's millions, "never worked a day in her life." Enter: stay-at-home moms vs. working moms, a.k.a. The Mommy Wars Remixed, Reloaded, and Blown Totally Out Of Proportion.

Somehow, Rosen's charge that the stinking-rich Romney, who raised five now-grown sons in her many houses with her husband's many millions, probably isn't the best person to advise anybody, much less her stinking-rich husband, about the economic concerns of American women, got turned into a referendum on how Democrats have contempt for stay-at-home moms. Romney, backed by a rabid gang of conservative pundits and a bunch of emotionally distracted stay-at-home moms, made quick work of setting up a Twitter account to tell the entire world that raising five kids is work.

Um . . . duh.

Of course it's hard work to raise children—whether you do it full-time at home or with a full-time job out of the house. But really, are we supposed to think Ann Romney can identify with *and help shape policy for* mothers in this economic climate— mothers raising children while struggling to find cash for food, clothing, housing, education, and transportation? I don't care if Ms. Ann was on her knees scrubbing her kitchen floors every other day and changing all of her kids' dirty diapers on her own: when you have *millions* in the bank, your worries are NOT the worries of a mother struggling and juggling on an everyday woman's salary (still significantly lower than men's—about 68 cents for black women for every dollar a white man makes, to be exact). A millionaire wife/mother's worries are NOT those of a married stay-at-home mom paying bills with her man's common, everyday salary.

The millionaire mother does not have to walk on the edge, wondering what will happen if a venture capital firm like Romney's Bain Capital comes along, dismantles her boss's company, eliminates jobs, and makes paychecks—livelihoods— disappear. . . .

The millionaire mother does not have to study the bank account and wonder how she's going to scrape up the rent, pay the light bill, buy the babies a $2.98 gallon of milk and fork over $4 a gallon to fill up the broke down car to get to work and the kids' doctor appointments and after-school activities on nothing but pennies and a desperate prayer to sweet baby Jesus. . . .

The millionaire mother does not have to let her baby wear the same wet diaper all day and into the evening because she's got to make that expensive pack of diapers last. . . .

The millionaire mother hasn't a clue what it's like to have your phone ring off the hook from sunup to can't see with bill collectors threatening you with foreclosure and electricity shut-offs and phone disconnections and credit score decimation. . . .

The millionaire mother has no idea what it's like to get sick and have to stay that way because you can't afford a simple doctor's appointment to figure out what the hell is wrong with you in the first place, much less the health insurance you need to fix whatever ails you or your babies. . . .

The millionaire mother can't begin to fathom what it's like to say to your child, "I know you want to play soccer, baby, but mommy doesn't have the registration and uniform fees," or, "I know you want to go on the school field trip, but mommy doesn't have the $12 you need to go to the museum," or "I know your tooth hurts but mommy doesn't have the money for the dentist this week," or "I know you want to eat three meals a day but I need you to eat really good at school because I don't know when I'll have money for breakfast and dinner." . . .

Yes, being a stay-at-home mom is work, but the true heavy lifting comes from minimizing the physical, mental, and emotional toll of raising babies without benefit of knowing where your next dollar is coming from, or even if your guaranteed dollar can stretch far and wide enough to make ends meet—something Ann Romney knows nothing about.

That's all to say that Rosen's comments weren't about working moms vs. stay-at-home moms; Rosen was talking about a woman married to a multimillionaire who had the benefit of *choosing* to stay at home to take care of/enjoy her children without a care in the world about how she'd feed, clothe, educate, and house them. Turning her words into a War on Women/stay-at-home vs. working moms argument is, while politically savvy, realistically out of touch with the masses.

I will say this much: Romney, who was trailing President Obama by the double digits amongst women voters, was genius for seizing on this mock "controversy" to pit women against each other, raise money for his presidential bid, and mask the fact that most people with vaginas and half a brain cell can't stand him and his political party right now because of their stance on reproductive health care, birth control, abortion, the economy, and the dismantling of the very safety net that means the difference, literally, between life and death for poor children.

But are we women really this politically naive that we'd toss our valuable vote into the ring of a man who neither understands nor gives two crap-filled diapers about what mothers want? What mothers need? Are we really so politically stupid that we'd let this man, his rich wife and their equally rich and out of touch cronies distract us from the real issues while we bicker and get all emo over who works harder—women who work solely in the home vs. women who hold down full-time jobs outside the home? When, exactly, do we mothers come together and demand politicians—whether Republican or Democrat, rich or poor, black or white—get down to the real issues that affect us mothers? When do we stop arguing over stupid shit and start exercising our political might to effect *real* change?

Please understand: Rosen vs. Romney is not a real fight. The back and forth is silly, and we mothers—and our children—can't afford to be distracted by it. Aside from it being disingenuous, it's incredibly insulting that the Romneys and the GOP would think we could be so easily tricked into taking our eyes off the political ball—a ball that, up to this point, we've been watching incredibly closely, for our own sakes. For the sake of our babies. We've been politically smarter than we've ever been; let's not get dumb and numb now.

Here's a challenge: forget about what Hilary Rosen said or what Ann Romney tweeted or how much money Mitt Romney raised when he scratched up The Mommy Wars by pitting stay-at-home moms vs. working moms. Instead, tell me in the comments section what you would like your next president to deliver to women—mothers—over the next four years. Tell the world what we women and mothers need and how our next president can get it to us. Let's take this election seriously—and, as the majority of this country, have our say. —*APRIL 2012*

MOTHER LOVE

CHAPTER 65

I'll Always Love My Mama

I 'M NOT SURE what made me think about her today. I was in the grocery store, smelling the overpriced strawberries, when my mother suddenly popped into my mind. It happens like that, you know. I'll be doing something absolutely mundane, and there she'll be, standing in the bathroom mirror of my childhood home, putting on her lipstick and adjusting her church hat; or standing over me and my Dad, watching us eat that extra sweet potato pie she baked just for us, because she knew we wouldn't be able to keep our hands off the two she made for Thanksgiving dinner; or singing a silly song to my Mari, which, even loud and off-key, always managed to make my then-baby girl fall fast asleep. Sometimes, the memories make me giggle a little. Sometimes, I can't quite control the tears, and I'm blinded by overwhelming sadness.

A lot of times, I just miss her so.

Bettye went away from here six years ago—suddenly, surprisingly, heart-achingly. Mari was three, and so she couldn't quite understand, really, why she wouldn't be able to lie in her Gamma's arms anymore. Lila was barely two months old, and so all she has is a few pictures of my mom holding her in her arms, nuzzling Lila's fat cheeks. I was a young mother, trying to figure out how to raise two girlpies and be a good wife and hold down a challenging magazine gig and write books and run a household and live a fulfilled life. None of us was ready for her to go. We needed her.

I needed her.

Still do.

I didn't always appreciate the mother that Bettye Millner was. She was old-school strict and a little mean and definitely one of those moms who thought children were to be seen, not heard. She reveled in making her kids do chores (I spent so much time scrubbing, vacuuming, and doing laundry during weekend high school events that I seriously considered changing my name to Cinderella). She chauffeured my brother, Troy, and me to church every Sunday, faithfully and with a smile. And most certainly, Bettye believed that any child who stepped out of line had a sound whooping coming right to 'em (her weapon of choice: a fresh, thin, sturdy switch from the tree in the front yard). She was tart-tongued and quick to tell you about yourself—fiercely protective and ridiculously private (she's somewhere on the other side clutching her pearls over me writing this blog about her, I'm sure!). And she prayed for us even when we didn't know it—even when we didn't deserve it. Especially when we needed it.

I expected her to be a similar kind of grandmother—to apply those strict, old-school traits to the way she would love my babies. But she was different with them—all googly and sweet and swooning. She would snatch Mari right out of my arms before she or I could get through the door, and rush her away to a room full of gifts, and a plate full of food, and a VCR full of kid movies just waiting for her grandbaby. She'd read to her and sing to her and talk to her and welcome Mari to talk back. She'd dress up her grandbaby and sport her down the church aisle *America's Next Top Model*-style, showing her off to anyone with eyes. And she'd fall asleep with Mari snuggled next to her in her bed, my father banished to the basement couch to make room for the little girl child she loved so.

And just as she revealed a different side of Bettye as grandmother, my mom revealed a different, softer side of herself to me, too. Suddenly, we became fellow moms: rather than tell me what to do, she encouraged me to do what I thought was right; instead of holding her secrets close, she shared them with the hope that they would help me be a better mom; rather than reprimand me for my childcare decisions, she trusted my judgment. I'll never forget the day when I came to her, distraught because someone very close to us criticized my decision to keep breastfeeding Mari past six months. Honestly, I expected her to agree; after all, what self-respecting, black working mom kept her ninny in a baby's mouth past a few months when there was work to do and baby formula at the ready?

"Mari is your baby," she insisted when I came to her, overwhelmed and a little mad at the judgmental mom who questioned my decision. "You're not ever going to hear me questioning how you're raising your child. You're going to make mistakes all of us did before you, and many will after you. You do what's right for you."

What I would do to have her here. To order. To direct. To encourage. And pray for me and mine. There are so many things that I wish she could see—Mari and Lila's fierce competitive spirit on the soccer field, the rows of A's on their report cards. I know she would love Lila's mischievousness and Mari's curiousness. She'd hang their artwork up on her refrigerator, and brag about her grandbabies to her friends, and sit them right up there in the front pew so they could pay attention to the preacher, and the other deaconesses could give them mints and pinches on their cheeks. And my mother would be overwhelmed by my daughters' beauty, proud of the young ladies they're becoming. Excited about who they'll be.

I do wish, too, that she were still here so that my daughters could see firsthand the incredible woman their grandmother was.

We are all missing out on something special now that Bettye Millner is gone.

I'll tell Mari and Lila about her though, to keep her fresh in their memories.

And I'll wait for her to come to me again a lovely, sweet, heart-breaking vision in my mind. —*MAY 2012*

CHAPTER 66

The Women Who Helped Raise Me & The BFFs Who Show My Girlpies How to Be

MY MOTHER HAD a tight clique of girlfriends who made her happy: they laughed together, cried together, fellowshipped together, bowled together, cooked together, sat in the deaconess pews together and, above all else, prayed together. Their friendship sustained them. Propelled them. Gave these mothers, wives, lovers . . . air.

And in the midst of their loving one another, each of my mother's friends—my aunties—loved me unconditionally. I have vivid memories of riding my tricycle on the concrete pathway ringing Sarah's house, dressed in matching outfits she sewed for her daughter, Sonya, and me, and sitting, too, between Sarah's legs as she weaved intricate cornrow styles into my hair. Her long fingernails would click together as she braided, much like they did when she played the organ early Sunday morning at St. John's Baptist Church, where she led the choirs in hosannas to the heavens.

I remember, too, saving up my pennies and nickels and dimes with the hope that Mommy would let me in on the Saturday night Pokeno action at Miss Tina's, who, if all went well during bowling league that afternoon, would often invite the whole crew of us over to her place for game night. The win wasn't necessarily the haul one could get from a successful Pokeno run, though; the draw of the night was over on her kitchen counter, perched under an elegant etched glass cake dish that housed her lemon pound cake—dense, spongy, tart, sweet, and unforgettably delicious.

If we weren't at Miss Tina's, you could usually find my mom and aunties at George Ragland's house. They affectionately called her "Rags." She made a point of sending the kids to the basement to listen to Stevie Wonder and Johnny Gill while the grown folk were left to their business. But she'd call us to the top of the stairs, though, when the chitlins and greens were finished—our bowls steaming and fresh, with extra hot sauce, thank you.

Miss Annette's house was the summer hangout spot: we kept her pool full and her grill hot, and she reveled in every splash, in every full stomach, in every giggle. Cynthia, the youngest of the crew, helped bridge the road between girlhood and young womanhood; from her, I could always count on an endless amount of support, particularly when my mother was sick, plus a shoulder to lean on and a sound listening ear. Cynthia's sister, Mrs. Lewis, was sweet and always ready with a kind word, and she revered the Lord. And Miss Lena, lovely, long, and fresh, with a singing voice that could simultaneously raise rafters and melt the hardest of hearts, taught us all how to be glamorous. So very glamorous.

I didn't realize it when I was little, but my mother's BFFs were curating valuable lessons for me—lessons on how to be. Watching them, I learned how to enjoy childhood but also how to be a lady. I learned, too, the value of friendship, of creating safe spaces for children, and of laughter. I lived for my aunties' hugs, their counsel, their approval, their truth. And they gave it—in spades. When I think of all the most significant moments in my life—my graduation, my wedding, the birth of my daughters, and the saddest day of my life, the burial of my mom—it is their faces that I see, their voices that I hear, their love that I feel.

This is what I'm hoping my daughters will remember about my best girlfriends when they get to be my age and have children of their own. I've made a point of, like my mother, curating my friends not only to fit my idea of friendship, but also to serve as an example for my girlpies. So when they visit with my dear friend and literary agent Victoria, they know humor, a deeply loving relationship, and protection, and get an up close look at the intricacies of a successful business. When they are blessed to be around my honey love, Akilah, they know adventure, free-spiritedness, and exploration (plus lots and lots of unapologetic grown-up fun!). When my girl Selassie is in the house, my girls get to see independence, sweetness, and pure beauty (plus, some of the best Ghanaian cooking in the Western Hemisphere), and Tina packs for them sensibility, organization, kindness, understanding, and finesse—the kind that comes with the most perfectly appointed home or that party you'll never, ever forget because she made it the most spectacular ever. From their auntie Angelou, they get that go-getter, entrepreneurial spirit and a fanatical love of and respect for nature.

In other words, just like I was blessed to have my mother's BFFs in my life, so, too, are my girlpies to have my best friends in theirs. And I'm so grateful for that. For them. I'll make that known, for sure, this Mother's Day, when we celebrate not only the mothers in our lives, but those who mother—who nurture and love and protect and give of themselves selflessly. —*MAY 2015*

CHAPTER 67

A Love Letter to the Woman Who Gave Me Away

I WAS 12 YEARS OLD when I found my adoption papers tucked in a metal box under my parents' bed. Too young to process alone the gravity of finding out my mother and father were not, in a biological sense, my mother and father, and way too scared to ask questions. My mother went to her grave not knowing that I knew and that I had kept her secret for more than 20 years. My dad came clean about it the day we buried the woman we both loved more than air. The details about how my parents came to adopt me are, to this day, scarce: my parents, having had two foster children, both boys, in their care, wanted a girl. And so they went to an orphanage in downtown Manhattan in search of a chocolate dewdrop of a baby and there I was, in a crib in a dark corner of the basement, chubby and curly-haired and giggly, arms outstretched toward the man who, with his wife, would love me and nurture me and care for me and pray for me for the rest of our days.

I don't talk about this much with my father; it's still an uneasy conversation to have. For him. For me. I don't want him to think for a second that I have some kind of grand scheme to go searching for my birth parents. Because really, I don't. I've known for what seems like forever that I have no interest in such folly; Bettye Millner is my mother and James Millner is my father and it is what it is and that's that. The heavens made this so. I see absolutely no reason to change the order of this thing.

Still, I always pause when I read stories like that of a 14-year-old facing manslaughter charges for neonaticide after police found a newborn, lifeless, in a plastic bag in the girl's room. Police were dispatched to the teen's house after her parents rushed her to the emergency room, bleeding from complications after having given birth. The girl's parents were clueless about the pregnancy, the birth, and the fact that their grandchild lay dead in their daughter's room either having died at birth or having been murdered.

I know that but for the grace of God, this could have been my fate. The woman who carried me in her belly for nine months easily could have been a teenager, frightened by the prospects of having to tell her parents that she was sexually active and with child—a child that she could not reasonably raise on her own. She could have been a young mother, hands already too full with the duty of raising a grip of kids she could barely feed and clothe and house back in the late '60s, when meaningful work and decent pay never seemed to come easy to women, especially black ones. She could have been raped and impregnated by a stranger—or maybe someone she knew. Someone she thought she loved and who was supposed to love her. She could have gotten pregnant in a lustful tryst with a man who was not her significant other—her belly full of the evidence of her infidelity. She could have been many things. Or none of these at all.

In my mind, though, I like to think of my birth mother as selfless. After all, she could have easily given birth to me in secret, ashamed and scared and in deep denial—a pain so searing that she saw no other way out but to take my life. Or she could have found herself on a table in the back room of an illegal abortion clinic, desperate for a way to end my life to save her own.

Instead, though, this woman gave me life by giving me away. She, or someone she knew, left me on a stoop, I'm told, somewhere down on Canal Street. As far as I know, there was no note—no details, no explanations, no promises. Just the expectation that the people who ran the orphanage would find a decent home for the chocolate dewdrop of a baby with the chubby cheeks and the curly hair, with arms outstretched, looking for a mom and dad to love me and nurture me and care for me and pray for me for the rest of my days.

It could be that my vision of what led me to that stoop on that day at that particular time—just four days before my parents came looking for me—is more romantic than the truth. Or maybe it's spot on. Whatever it is, I know this much is true: I am forever grateful to her, this woman who gave me life, for letting me live and loving me enough not only to want for me what she knew she couldn't provide but having the strength to find someone who could. It was a decision that led me to this specific place at this specific time—to a life filled with love and joy and peace and beauty.

What I'm sure she wanted for her baby girl. —*FEBRUARY 2011*

CHAPTER 68

Telling the Truth about Balancing Work & Motherhood

L ET'S JUST GET THIS on out the way: eff the *New York Post* for screaming from its front page that Chirlane McCray, wife of New York City mayor Bill de Blasio, is a "BAD MOM" for being 100 percent honest about how difficult it was for her to put aside her career for motherhood. Eff *The Post* so hard.

Yeah, I said it.

Because I remember.

There is the humongous belly and the swollen ankles and the weirdo cravings and, my God, the breathless, sleepless nights with body parts jerking and groaning and leaning each and every which way. And then there's the stretching and pushing and serrated knife-style searing pain that makes us feel like Jason or maybe Satan himself is tearing us limb from limb when we push a full human being from our loins.

And then, nine months after love is consummated and seed meets egg, finally, suddenly, there we are: somebody's mama. In those first moments we are ecstatic and exhausted, hopelessly, helplessly in love and completely, ridiculously effing clueless, feigning confidence and scared shitless that we will break them— our babies. We don't know what we're doing. The books, the classes, the regaled tales from the moms who've been there, done that, don't mean a damn thing.

There is only one thing that we know is true: we are mothers. And everything for us has changed.

Relationships morph. Time shifts. We are catching vomit in our hands and washing green projectile poop off our bedspreads and letting a little human gnaw our nipples with vice-gripping gums. We are not who we used to be. Even and especially when that's all some of us want.

That last part is true and fair and not at all uncommon. Indeed, it is human.

And so Chirlane's recollections about new motherhood in *New York* magazine are not only candid but ridiculously familiar. Any woman who's ever faced the awkward two-step that is work-life balance after kids knows this for sure:

> "I was 40 years old. I had a life. Especially with Chiara—will we feel guilt forever more?" Chirlane said of the birth of her first child, a daughter, in her New York magazine interview. "Of course, yes. But the truth is, I could not spend every day with her. I didn't want to do that. I looked for all kinds of reason not to do it. I love her. I have thousands of photos of her—every one-month birthday, two-month birthday. But I've been working since I was 14, and that part of me is me. It took a long time for me to get into 'I'm taking care of kids,' and what that means."

And you know what? That's real deal Holyfield, y'all. Dead right, all the way down to the bone. Chirlane's revelations about what it took to get her mind right behind being a mom and passionate about work sound a lot like the conversations you've had with your best girlfriends and your sisters and your coworkers when you kissed the babies and wiped the booties and fixed the bottles and secretly wished you were back in the office, doing the work and earning your keep and all up in the middle of the action. Nothing wrong with this.

So why did the *New York Post*, and, to a lesser extent, the *Daily News*, make Chirlane out to be some kind of god-awful human being for wanting to honor the 40 years of life she lived before she became a mom? Why is it so okay for a man to become a father and proudly hold on to every inch of who he is outside the home, but not so much for a woman?

Because here in America, where we scream "family values" from every rooftop and ballot box (but then move heaven and earth to deny the social safety nets necessary to help mothers and children who choose motherhood over jobs survive and thrive) there is no space for a lady to be both woman and mother. No room for bottles in the boardrooms or a power suit in the nurseries.

Well, isn't it time we call bullshit? Who says that in 2014, we should be all-the-way-good with a crappy, has-been, sensational rag like the *Post* painting motherhood with that stupid *Leave It to Beaver* brush?

Hello, *NY Post?* The '50s called—they want their stereotypical mom tropes back. The 21st century in its entirety wouldn't mind you returning those "black moms suck" labels, either. (Oh, please believe, I don't doubt for one second that Chirlane's deep, dark chocolate skin and those locs and those biracial children with the wild and woolly hair helped the *Post* editors along in their headline-picking process.)

Mayor de Blasio gets all the high fives and fist bumps for coming to his wife's defense and demanding the *Post* and the *News* issue an apology to his wife for their ridiculous headlines. "It suggests a tremendous misunderstanding of what it means to be a parent, what it means to be a mother," de Blasio said of the coverage in a hastily called news conference yesterday. "A lot of hardworking women in this city are offended," Mr. de Blasio added. "I think both the *Post* and the *Daily News* owe Chirlane an apology. I think they owe all of us an apology."

Indeed.

Full disclosure: I was a political and entertainment reporter for the *Daily News* for eight years back in the '90s, so I get the rush for the raucous front page and sensational headlines. But this here? Too far. Do better, y'all. At least try. Damn.

In the meantime, we here at *MyBrownBaby* certainly #StandWithChirlane and thank her not just for her candor but for using her platform as the First Lady of New York City to speak up on behalf of us moms. Us women. —*MAY 2014*

CHAPTER 69

My Biggest Competition Is THIS Woman. Who's Yours?

S HE GETS ON MY NERVES REALLY—this chick who's spent a lifetime making me feel wholly inadequate. Even when we were little, she made a point of showing me up—donning her fancy dresses and holding my Mom's hand while Mommy marched down the church aisle, bragging to anyone who would listen about that girl's straight As and her Honors Society kudos and her first chair flute status in the school band. She was cute. Never got into any trouble. Did exactly as she was told.

Perfect.

And that perfect girl grew up into the perfect teenager—went to college on a scholarship and started her own magazine and focused on becoming a journalist instead of on boys and partying and all the scary, ridiculous, fun experimenting college students do. And, of course, then she became the perfect woman—at least according to society's standards: a dutiful wife, a loving, attentive, doting-but-firm mom, and a career woman who excelled at her craft, holding down gigs as a political and then entertainment reporter before becoming a senior magazine editor and then national columnist and then the bestselling author of more than two dozen books.

In public, I'm proud of her for all she's accomplished and make a point of saying such, especially when everyone else is piling on, singing her praises—telling her she's fierce and fly and inspirational and sheer awesome.

But in private, she scares me. Her success is intimidating; no matter how hard I try, I find it hard to keep up with her frenetic pace. Her successes. And other peoples' expectations of her.

I am inspired by the best—the playwright August Wilson, the collagist Romare Bearden, the songstresses Jill Scott and Erykah Badu, the writers Dorothy West and J. California Cooper—all amazing artists who dedicated their talent to staying true to their culture and their people. They, I admire. But she? She makes me put my dukes up.

And I battle her every day.

She does make me stronger, you know. My fear of her success is a fantastic motivator. With her—and for her—I rise to the occasion, no matter how tired, no matter how insecure, no matter that my inner critic is constantly telling me, "Against her, you can't win."

Failure, you see, is not an option.

It never has been for this perfect child who became a perfect teenager who became the perfect woman.

See, I am her.

She is me.

And I consider me to be the biggest competition I know.

Not because I think I'm the best around—by any stretch.

But because I don't ever want to go backward—or to disappoint me, my biggest critic.

One of these days, maybe, I'll cut myself a break. But until that day comes, I'll keep on pushing, keep on striving, keep on achieving.

Keep on. —*APRIL 2014*

CHAPTER 70

The Working Mom's Survival Kit: 15 Ways to Make Life More Manageable

S EE, THE THING IS, every few months some celebrity or super CEO or magazine cover story questions whether women can "have it all" and everybody starts arguing about work-life balance and what it takes to have a career, raise kids, wrangle a man, and take time for self. While everyone is yammering on, I'm over here in the real world, tracking down working mom survival tips and trying to figure out forreal forreal if, between work, getting the kids situated at school, plotting and planning after-school activities, and keeping the house clean and the entire family fed, whether I'll be able to squeeze in a solid four hours of sleep oh, I don't know, next Tuesday. Who has time to philosophize about "having it all" when you're busy *doing* it all? *looks around, slowly raises hand* Not me, ma'am. Not me at all.

But I do give my busy kid/work/school/husband/home schedule a run for its money by putting a little bit more thought and care into its management. Holding down three kids, three jobs, three sports teams, a husband, and a laundry list of activities too numerous to count will help you learn some things. While my house is far—*far!*—from perfect, I do have a few tricks up my sleeve to maximize time, coordinate schedules, keep order in our home, and help make my job(s) juggling it all a little more easy. Here, 15 ways I make life more manageable as a working mom.

WORKING MOM SURVIVAL TIPS

1. **Take off the cape.** Recognize that you're not Superwoman and you can't do everything for everybody every time. Be realistic about what you can accomplish in the course of any given day, and say "no" to things that'll hang you up. Getting the kids to school and soccer practice, working eight hours, cooking dinner, helping with homework, and getting everyone in bed by a reasonable hour is more than enough for one day. When your girlfriend asks you to add in baking 10 pies for Wednesday Bible study, give her the number to a local bakery. That's what *they* do during the week. Not you.

2. **Get outfits together the night before.** Lay it all out, down to the earrings, shoes, and perfume you'll be wearing. Same for the kids. You'll be amazed how much time you save not having to stare into the closet during the morning rush.

3. **Delegate chores.** Yes, kids can do stuff. And they should understand early on that they, too, can contribute to the care and upkeep of your home. A 3-year-old can make up her bed and put toys away, a 7-year-old can clear the dinner table, a 10-year-old can fold laundry, and my 15-year-old, bless her heart, can cook dinner twice a week. Make chores a part of your child's daily responsibilities to free up some time for yourself.

4. **Do timed cleaning.** I mean, seriously: I just don't have hours every day to scrub the house from top to bottom. But I can do some damage on dirt if I dedicate 15 minutes of uninterrupted cleaning. I get out my bucket of cleaning products, turn on A Tribe Called Quest, set the timer on my smartphone, and deep dive into the bathroom on one day, the living room on another, my bedroom a day after

that. Once the timer goes off, whatever room I was power cleaning is sparkling. And then I leave it alone. Period.

5. **Plan out meals for the week.** Nothing is more frustrating to me than trying to figure out at the last minute what we're going to eat for dinner. Plus, not planning leads to poor eating choices for us—like, "ugh, I don't have time to go to the grocery store and cook dinner, so let's get fast food!" Instead, on Sunday, I plot out what we'll be eating for the next five days, down to the sides, and then I head to the grocery store. Bonus: I spend less at the supermarket when I walk in focused and I leave with only what I need.

6. **Cook several meals in one day.** Toss some chicken and sausage on the grill, whip up a pan of lasagna, and roll a few meatballs around your pot and you've got the main dish for at least five days if you plan it right. Freeze what you'll be serving toward the end of the week, and putting dinner on the table after a busy day becomes a cinch.

7. **Have "stupid dinner."** At least one night out of the week, everybody is charged with fending for themselves and eating something that doesn't require anything more than heating up a plate of leftovers in the microwave or scrambling a few eggs. This requires no thought or time, everyone leaves the table full and I get to go to bed with my sanity intact (at least for that night!).

8. **Make lunch the night before.** Really, the last thing I need is to be running around the kitchen at 6 a.m., tossing juice boxes and PB&J sandwiches into paper bags. Instead, right after dinner (while the girls are cleaning the kitchen!), I spread out onto the counter everything I need to prepare their lunches and I have at it. This way, I've bought myself an extra 15 minutes to get out the door in the morning, and they can grab their lunch and be on their way.

9. **Put yourself on daily social media time-outs.** I use the Self-Control app to block myself from Facebook, Twitter, and other sites I'm addicted to. This gives me hours of focused work time without the distraction of the latest crazy cat video, browsing for cute shoes, or arguments about who's hotter: Idris Elba or Michael Ealy.

10. **Open email at a set time.** If I'm checking email every five minutes, I'm allowing myself to get pulled into 20 different directions by focusing on the requests of others instead of my own work. I open my email once in the morning, once in the afternoon, and once before the workday is over, and give myself 20 minutes to answer it.

11. **Call on the village.** Asking for help is not a sign of weakness. We all need it. Barter things like babysitting and errand runs, take turns with team parents getting the kids to sporting activities, and styling your daughters' hair or running the boys to the barbershop. And when you need to talk it out, let your friends know you may need a sympathetic ear or a shoulder to cry on. Be the same for them and this work-life balance thing feels a little more manageable.

12. **Don't sweat the small stuff.** So what if your kid is the last one of your friends' kids to be potty trained. Who cares that your coworker came in late yesterday or that PTA mom made homemade cupcakes and you bought yours from the grocery store. Nobody will remember that mess a year from now. Or even a month out. Or tomorrow. Move on: you have more important things to focus on.

13. **Stop second-guessing and beating up on yourself.** Once you make a decision, trust that you're doing what's right for you and your family. And if it doesn't work out the way you planned or expected, that's okay, too. No need to feel bad about it. After all, you did what you thought was right. And that's what matters.

14. **Love on your babies and remind them that they matter.** Juggling school and work and everything in between can leave us harried and, let's be real, a little crazy, which turns into barking orders and making demands and forgetting, sometimes, that the best kind of encouragement comes from a warm hug, a kiss on the cheek, and a reminder that above all else, you love your kids. Take the time to play with and bond with your kids; they'll appreciate it, and so will you.

15. **Make time for you.** Get in 30 minutes of exercise because it's good for your body. Get your nails done because it's good for your sanity. Pray and meditate because it's good for your soul. If you don't nurture yourself, you can't possibly take care of everyone else. —*OCTOBER 2014*

CHAPTER 71

That Mommy Smell

MY GOD, when Mari was born, I was mesmerized by her scent. I mean, I'd find myself just burying my nose in her neck and her belly and her shiny little toes and inhaling and thinking that she was absolutely delicious. I don't know if it was the baby powder or the baby lotion or the baby soap or the Dreft or just the baby or a combination of all of them together, but it was an elixir—an addictive, yummy elixir that would send me swooning.

Mari and I were talking about this the other day, while I was whipping up dinner. She looked up lazily from her homework and started grilling me about my favorite colors and songs and sounds and smells, and I got totally stuck on describing that baby smell of hers, and then dutifully shined the light back on her:

Me: So, what's your favorite smell?

Mari: Well, I like the way sunscreen smells—it reminds me of the beach. And I love the beach.

Me: I know that's the truth.

Mari: And I like the smell of the Christmas tree early in the morning, especially when we're ripping open presents.

Me: Mmm . . . I love that smell, too.

Mari: Ooh, and cinnamon cookies in the oven—that smell makes my mouth water.

Me: Oh yeah!

Mari: And I really love the smell of laundry detergent, especially Tide. It makes me chew my tongue.

Me: Weird. You were digging laundry detergent even when you were in my belly. I used to want to eat Tide. But that's a whole 'nother story.

Mari: I love the way you smell, too. You have that mommy smell—it's there whenever I hug you. It makes me want to hug you more.

Now, who knew? I mean, I wear a special lotion from Bath & Body Works that keeps the proactive ash at bay, but also happens to smell pretty nice, and Nick really likes it because it's a fresh, clean, earthy scent. But I didn't realize it made Mari a little loopy, too. Imagine that: My baby-girl-turned-big-girl, whose baby smell has been soundly replaced by deodorant and Renuzit sports spray (to keep the funk of 1,000 soccer games at bay), thinks I smell delicious, too.

I've arrived, you know. I remember thinking the same thing about my mom, too. She used to use this special lotion by Fashion Fair that she could only purchase at the cosmetics counter at Macy's, and no one in the house was allowed to use it but her. It was expensive, see—like, $15 a bottle, which was a big deal for her working-class budget—so the only one who could smell like that Fashion Fair lotion was the person willing to splurge 15 ducats to wear it.

I suppose that's what made it special.

And when my mom passed away, her scent seemed to fill

every crevice of the home she and my Dad shared; it was on the blankets and in her closets and on her scarves and church hats and purses. Her jewelry, even.

Believe it or not, almost 10 years after she went on to fly with the angels, the box in which I keep her jewelry still smells like that lotion—like my mom. I try not to open it too much, for fear that her scent will wear off. But on special occasions—Mother's Day, mommy's birthday, the anniversary of her death, the rare occasions when she visits me in my dreams—I'll open up that box and breathe in deep and remember my mommy's Mommy Smell.

How amazing, then, to find out I have one of my own—a signature scent that reminds my daughter of me.

My embrace.

My love.

How delicious. —*JANUARY 2012*

CHAPTER 72

How Mommy Got Her Groove Back

L ET ME JUST GO AHEAD and put this on out there: I can't dance.
I mean, if you put on, say, Stevie Wonder's "As," Earth,
Wind & Fire's "September," maybe some Jay-Z or a little old-
school Hip Hop, I can drop it like it's on fire. But when it comes
to organized routines—choreographed dances that require coordi-
nated movement, especially with others—I'm about as graceful as
an elephant in a conga line. It's. Not. Pretty.

So when my sister-in-law/BFF Angelou invited me to a local
African dance class, you can imagine how quick I was to run
through my mental calendar to come up with a gang of reasons
why I just didn't have any time over the next year to make it there.
But Ang is really persuasive. And she offered to drive. And give
me a glass of Riesling when class was over.

Well, have drink? Will travel.

Our instructor, Sauda, promised to be gentle. And she was.
While the drummers beat an incredible rhythm, she led us through
a series of warm-ups and then slowly introduced us to a series of
age-old traditional West African dances—a bit of Manjani, a little
Lamba, some Kuku. I'll tell you this much: exercise gurus Billy
Blanks, Donna Richardson, and Richard Simmons ain't got nut-
hin' on Sauda, you hear me? Every pound of the drum required a
different movement from a different body part; every inch of me
was bending and stretching and bowing and gyrating and kicking
and leaping in ways I never thought possible. I had quite the time

266

trying to keep up, too; when Sauda said go left, I went right; by the time I got to the bend, everyone else was soaring through the air.

It was ugly, I tell you.

But then the cooldown came, and Sauda slowed down and the drummers, Sekou and Jerome, hit a smoothed-out beat, and suddenly, I could breathe again (kinda). And then Sauda instructed each of us to open our arms wide and slowly wrap them around ourselves while we swayed to the drums. This, she said, is a hug from me to you, from you to me, from we to we, positive energy filled with love and light. And then, mid-hug, she encouraged us to pat ourselves on the back, because if no one else does, at least you can, she added. That hug, those pats, are always available to you. Use them to help yourself remember just how valuable and beautiful and wonderful you are.

And right there, in that moment, with my own arms holding me tight, in a roomful of fellow dancers, each of them supportive, interesting, smart, fun, committed moms and wives, I knew that no matter how wack my dance skills, that class was where I wanted and needed to be. Each of us needs it like we need air. I was getting in some (much-needed!) exercise and learning the beauty of a continent's cultural expression, and, most importantly, getting in much-deserved me-time, the incredibly freeing feeling that comes when no one is asking you to do stuff, or focus on them, or put aside your needs to lead the team. That time when it's all about y-o-u and y-o-u alone.

I've been taking that class for almost a year; now Tuesdays and Fridays are my dance nights, and everybody in the house is on notice that it's just not a good idea to try to book Mommy's schedule between 7:30 p.m. and 8:30 p.m. when I'm supposed to be in class. Oh, you can try. But you might just get your little feelings hurt.

Let me make it to class, though, make it to my hug, and it's virtually guaranteed that I'll spread the love.

Ashé! —*NOVEMBER 2008*

CHAPTER 73

There's No Place like Home

T HEY COME EVERY AFTERNOON with book bags flying and their Converse stomping the front lawn and their maniacal little giggles rushing into the still air, oblivious to what has been done while they were gone, and what is still to be done, too. I am usually clutching my to-do list to my chest, with way too many to-dos still unchecked, a little frantic. It is rush hour at the Chiles household, and my second, third, fourth, and fifth jobs are about to begin: homework tutor, chauffeur, cook, bathtub wrangler, midnight seductress. I want to hide. Or call in reinforcements. Or better, just take the doggone day off.

My husband, God bless him, notices these things, and, on occasion, takes pity on me. Sometimes, that mercy comes in the form of takeout dinner, or a break from after-dinner kitchen duty, or all-access to the bedroom remote and my trusty pillow. And when he's feeling especially benevolent, Nick, the editor-in-chief of the travel magazine *Odyssey Couleur*, tosses a travel junket my way—an all-expenses-paid trip to a place where laundry rooms and homework are nonexistent, somebody else cooks and drives and cleans, and I can just chill, sans interruption or obligation. In return, I write a story about my trip for his magazine, but this is small payment.

The. Trips. Are. Glorious.

I started writing this *MyBrownBaby* blog from the shores of the Alabama Gulf Coast, where Nick has sent me for a four-day respite. I'm posted up in a well-appointed, three-bedroom, two-bathroom condo, spotless with granite countertops in the eat-in kitchen, a grand king-sized bed in a master bedroom with a huge deck overlooking the bay, and a flat-screen TV equipped with CNN, HGTV, and an endless loop of Bravo's *Project Runway* and *The Real Housewives of Atlanta*. There is no laundry room (not one that I have to use, anyway). All dirty dishes are being left on the tables at fine restaurants all across town for someone else to clean. There are no dirty little brown girl booties in my Jacuzzi bathtub. And nobody is smacking me on my shoulder, waking me from a sound slumber to tell me their throat is sore, or they're so parched that surely they're going to die of thirst, or the little boy from *Where the Wild Things Are* just might be hiding out in the closet.

There is only peace here.

I'm finding it in the gentle whisper of the wind tickling the ocean just outside my window, a heavenly early morning alarm, for sure. And on the deck of sailboats, while I teeter dangerously over the edge to feel the water spray against my face and watch the dolphins play tag and beg for the croacker and jewelfish and eel and shrimp that the captain's caught and tossed their way. There is peace, too, in the wildlife refuge I hiked this morning, where Hurricane Ivan had his way, but somehow, the beauty of this land and all its inhabitants remained steady, stunning, and sure. And I found plenty of satisfaction at the bottom of the gigantic bowl of bread pudding and homemade whipped cream I just demolished, without worry or apology.

I wore red shoes and red lipstick, and sexy dresses and curls in my hair and drank mojitos and slurped down raw oysters with plenty of horseradish and hot sauce, and flitted about without a care in the world. And then I came back to this big ol' condo, and turned on the TV, and lay across the bed and, well, did the mom punk out. I'm longing for my family, wishing that Mari and Lila could have held the slimy fish in their hands and giggled when the dolphin dipped in and out of the water, and that Mazi could have walked along the beach and tasted the plethora of shrimp prepared in more ways than even Forrest Gump and his friend Bubba ever could have imagined. And I am longing to fall asleep in Nick's arms, to lay my head on his chest and let the thump of his heartbeat soothe me like no ocean waves ever can.

I'm longing, simply, for life—my simple family life.

All of a sudden, this three-bedroom condo seems cavernous— too dark and a little scary. As I sit here with every light in this place blazing, CNN blaring the same Obama/McCain/America-as-We-Know-It-Is-Coming-to-an-End stories it's had on repeat for the past three weeks, I'm reminded of a passage in bell hooks's picture book, *Homemade Love*, a bedtime favorite in our house, about a little girlpie whose parents love her hard and strong. At night, they tuck their little honey bun chocolate dewdrop in, and she snuggles under her covers in her bed, in her house, safe, satisfied, and surrounded by unconditional love. And when she falls asleep, this is on her mind:

> Memories of arms that hold me
> Hold me tight
> No need to fear the dark place
> 'Cause everywhere is home

Really, there's no place like home, is there? I mean, I'm so very grateful for this me-time; every last one of us hardworking moms craves it deserves it. I also know that so many of us aren't blessed to have these kinds of getaway opportunities come their way, that work gets in the way and family gets in the way and busy gets in the way and, yes, we get in our own way.

But the peace and solitude I found here in Alabama can't compare to the peace and solitude I find in my chaotic, messy, love-filled home. There, with arms that hold me tight, I have no need to fear the dark place.

Because at my house, everywhere is home. —*JULY 2009*

ACKNOWLEDGMENTS

For God, who keeps opening windows for me when it seems all doors are closed—without His grace, I am surely nothing.

For my husband, and darling daughters Mari and Lila, and my son Mazi: it is for you that I do what I do—thank you for your constant encouragement, support, and love, which make each of my words tumble easily to the page, even the stubborn ones. With you all and Teddy by my side, all things are possible.

For my Daddy, James Millner, and my brother, Troy Millner: thank you for loving me hard and strong—you both helped mold me into the woman I am today.

For my hearts, Selassie, Tina, Akilah, Ida, and Joyce, the women who keep me grounded, listen to my crazy stories, and fill our time together with unconditional sisterhood, love, and unapologetic honesty: thank you for the honor of allowing me to call you friends. With each of you by my side, I can be . . . me.

For Victoria Sanders, my agent extraordinaire and my heart sister: thank you for keeping me working and constantly challenged—you are my everything.

For the *MyBrownBaby* audience: thank you for inspiring some of the best, most important writing I've done in my entire career—the kind that inspires, the kind that gets to the heart of the matter, the kind that fully embraces the beauty that is us, black mothers.

And finally, for my partner Doug Seibold: thank you for the deft touch, the deep understanding of why publishing books in Technicolor is not only important, but necessary, and especially for your constant source of inspiration for this writer and, now, head of my own imprint: truly, it is a joy to work with you. Thank you for teaching and growing me up in this industry; every writer should have the great fortune of having a mentor like you. Thank you for being my partner and showing me the way.

ABOUT THE AUTHOR

New York Times-bestselling author Denene Millner is an award-winning journalist who has worked in the entertainment, parenting, social media, and book publishing fields. A former *Parenting* magazine columnist, she has penned 27 books, among them *Act Like a Lady, Think Like a Man*, co-written with Steve Harvey; *Around the Way Girl*, a memoir with actress Taraji P. Henson; *Early Sunday Morning*, a children's picture book; and *The Vow*, the novel on which the hit Lifetime original movie *With this Ring* was based. She also is the founder and editor of MyBrownBaby.com, an award-winning, critically acclaimed blog that examines the intersection of parenting and motherhood through the multicultural experience. She has contributed entertainment writing to *Essence*, *Ebony*, *Redbook*, and *Family Circle*; her extensive broadcast experience includes appearances on the *Today* show, *The Meredith Vieira Show*, the *Rachael Ray Show*, HLN, MSNBC, and NPR. She lives in Atlanta with her husband and their two daughters.

ALSO BY DENENE MILLNER

ISBN: 978-1-57284-211-3 | $17.95

Love and family give a little girl courage
to stand up straight and sing her best
on Sunday morning.